I'm not a numbers person

How to make good decisions in a data-rich world

Dr Selena Fisk

MACMILLAN

First published in 2023 by Major Street Publishing Pty Ltd

First published in India 2023 by Macmillan
an imprint of Pan Macmillan Publishing India Private Limited
707 Kailash Building
26 K. G. Marg, New Delhi 110001
www.panmacmillan.co.in

Pan Macmillan, The Smithson, 6 Briset Street, Farringdon, London EC1M 5NR
Associated companies throughout the world
www.panmacmillan.com

ISBN 978-93-95624-93-0

1 3 5 7 9 8 6 4 2

Internal design by Production Works
Printed in India by Gopsons Papers Pvt. Ltd., Noida

Praise for *I'm Not a Numbers Person*

Data can be intimidating for many people. Fisk's book provides a valuable lifeline to anyone who aspires to start using data on a more regular basis but doesn't know where to begin or how to get started. She lays out the key data concepts and skills you'll need to initiate your journey into the numbers with confidence.
Brent Dykes, Chief Data Storyteller, Analytics Hero, LLC

Thanks to technology, love it or not, data is everywhere. This book serves as an essential guide that helps all develop comfort and confidence in not just understanding and navigating data better, but in embracing and leveraging it in ways that help us improve the way we live and work. A must-read!
Jake Sapirstein, Founder and Head of Strategy, LiftCentro

In this book Selena shows you exactly how to integrate data and storytelling in a succinct, easy-to-understand and practical way. I cannot recommend this book enough – it is a must-read for all leaders in all areas of business.
Winitha Bonney OAM, Diversity and Inclusion Expert

I'm Not a Numbers Person is the book you want every person in your company to read to have better conversations about the business. Whether you lead a team, need to find more customers, or want more confidence in your decisions, this book is your go-to resource. CEOs and HR leaders – you need to get *I'm Not a Numbers Person* for every employee!
Geraldine Ree, Experienced SVP, author and speaker

'Emotional' and 'engaging' are not words commonly associated with analytical books, but Selena's storytelling method breathes life into the numbers. *I'm Not a Numbers Person* is written in a way that encourages you to think and reflect on your own circumstances, then gives you the tools to develop your own abilities.
Ian Wiltshire, Chief Information Officer

Selena's work engages, inspires and challenges people in an authentic manner. Personnel in our organisation are richer for the opportunity to have experienced Selena's passionate message that is so relevant to contemporary business. We all now see our data stories, and those of our clients, as integral to business improvement and maximising impact.
Catherine Jackson, Director, Leopard Tree Consulting

Selena shares practical, thought-provoking insights in her book that challenge individuals and teams to engage with data to inform decisions and to tell the story of the business: past, present and future. I highly recommend this book to both aspiring and experienced leaders who want to accelerate their leadership and management capacity.
Liam Kelly, CEO, Southern Cross Motel Group

I'm not a numbers person

Contents

Introduction 1

Chapter 1: Why data literacy? 13

Chapter 2: Understanding numbers 39

Chapter 3: Visualising data 83

Chapter 4: Establishing trends 105

Chapter 5: Making decisions and taking action 129

Conclusion 157

Glossary 161

References 165

About the author 173

Acknowledgements 175

Introduction

> 'In today's business environment, organizations accumulate massive amounts of data, and their ability to make informed decisions and drive business performance depends in a part on their acumen and competency in analyzing these data and converting them into actionable insights.'
>
> (Daradkeh, 2021)

My friend Michael runs two photography companies and has done so for the last 10 years. He is a self-professed nerd and loves everything tech related. I was recently talking to him about his business – about the progress he was making, and how he makes financial decisions. It surprised me when this spreadsheet loving, numbers-mad person told me that, even though he tracks every dollar earned and spent to the cent, he is not sure what to do with all the other data he has access to. He regularly uses Google Analytics to look at how his website is performing, where his customers come from and how long they spend looking at different pages; but he admitted he doesn't actually know what he should be paying attention to, or what to do about it. He says it is 'interesting' information, but he doesn't do anything with it.

At the opposite end of the spectrum, there are organisations that pride themselves on being data-driven. One example is Expedia, a company that has access to, and uses, extensive amounts of data (Melendez, 2015). The 2015 merger of Expedia and Orbitz led to the development of a huge travel organisation that holds and collects millions of complex data points – meaning that, as of 2017, Expedia needed approximately 150 data scientists on staff to cater for, and harness, the huge amounts of information (Reuters Events, 2017). This data is used to do things like predict user behaviour, provide recommended hotel offerings and organise options based on ratings, cost or duration. Over the last two years, individual staff, and Expedia as a whole, have promoted and shared their data-driven culture with others (Sharma, 2021) as they feel it has given them a competitive edge – that it sets them apart in understanding consumer behaviour.

Irrespective of where you sit on the spectrum of data and evidence use – from not knowing what to use or how to use it, through to capitalising on data – and regardless of whether you are a solopreneur, a small business owner, an emerging leader or in an executive leadership role, life in the 21st century dictates that you need to know your numbers and use them to enhance your impact. Increasingly, executives and board members around the world are held personally responsible for knowing the data – meaning that this understanding helps minimise and mitigate risk not only for businesses but for individuals. Whether you're organising your home budget and feeding your kids, or running a multinational, multi-million-dollar organisation, it is no longer sufficient to say 'but I'm not a numbers person' and believe that it is someone else's job to keep track of the numbers. We all need to be data literate and able to ask the right questions at the right time.

Data is all around us, and the quantities of data that we have access to are increasing at an extraordinary rate. Masses of data have been growing exponentially for the last few decades; however, finding a consensus on just how much data is out there is quite difficult. In a publication by the World Economic Forum, Jeff Desjardins (founder and editor at Visual Capitalist) estimated that by 2020, there would be '40 times more bytes [of data] than there are stars in the observable universe.' That amount of data is incomprehensible (and, to be honest, I don't even really understand how or where all that information is stored)! But what we do know is this increased volume of data needs increased storage space. The largest data centre in the world is currently being built in the Nevada desert. While the average data centre occupies approximately 100,000 square feet, the new centre – Switch's Citadel Campus – will contain 7.3 million square feet of data storage (Zhang, 2020). The data-verse in which we find ourselves is continuing to expand exponentially.

Whether you realise it or not, you are generating and being exposed to more data than ever before. While this might sound daunting, it means you have more evidence than ever before to inform your decisions. If you weren't great at maths at school, or you feel that you need to get better with numbers (either for your current role or to move up to the next level), this is the book for you.

No longer is it enough to settle for numbers not being your strength, or hope someone else will analyse and act on the data for you. We desperately need more humans on this planet who fundamentally understand and respond to the evidence they have, as well as significant numbers of people who can critically engage in conversations about data and numbers and use them in a way that informs what they do.

How do you use data?

Like the development of any skill, everyone fits somewhere into a continuum of data use – from no understanding and use through to highly effective and reflective practice. Along this continuum, people fit into one of six different levels of skill and understanding in using evidence, and the further they move up the levels, the greater impact they can have as a result of using and responding to the data. As shown in figure 0.1, as you progress along the continuum of the amount of data that you use, you can have an increasing impact within your sphere of influence. These categories apply regardless of your home and work life situation, as they do to the teams you work in and lead, and the organisation you work for. The six levels are: unconscious, conscious, casual, aware, active and reflective. Like any new skill, with time and effort, we all have the potential to move up through the levels.

Figure 0.1: Levels of data use versus impact

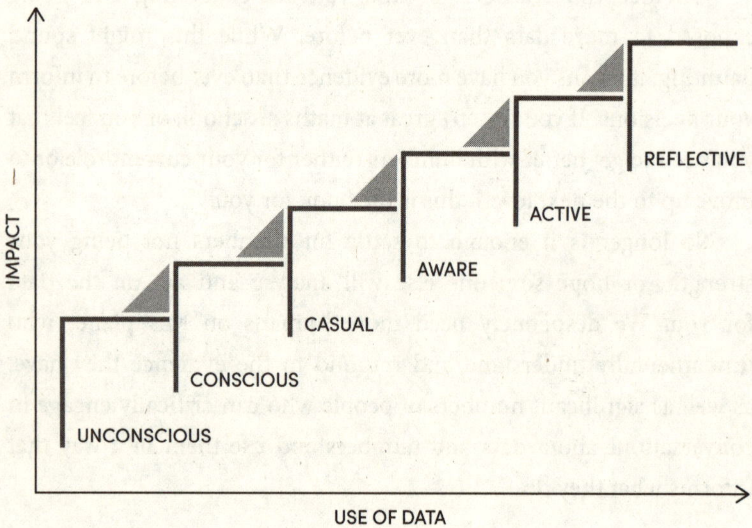

As you read through the explanations of each level on the following pages, think about which of these categories you fit into. Which description resonates with you the most? What about your colleagues and members of your team – where would you position them? Ultimately, the position that you are currently in doesn't really matter – what is important is to reflect on your current use of evidence and the impact this has, and remember that you can and will progress up the levels if you wish to.

Unconscious

Unconscious data and evidence users are genuinely oblivious to the data in the world around them. Not too many of these people exist in our world now; but if you know someone who still withdraws money from the bank with their chequebook, doesn't own a smartphone or isn't connected to the internet, they are probably an unconscious user. They are blissfully unaware of the data collected on citizens, data analysts' roles in organisations, and the existence of data science degrees.

If you have picked up this book, chances are you are not in this category. The unconscious user doesn't know what they don't know, therefore they have little interest in learning about numbers in this way. They are unaware that there's a whole other world out there where numbers rule.

Conscious

Conscious data users have a limited understanding of the numbers and what they mean. Unlike *unconscious* users, they are at least cognisant of the fact that data exists.

Conscious users might call Mark Zuckerberg's social networking behemoth 'The Facebook', or worry about people stealing all their money if they get a bank card. They know there is something else out there, they just don't know much about it.

Because they don't have a deep understanding of it, people in this stage are often quite fearful of data. They might have heard something negative, or latched onto a particular risk about a data breach – and because they don't understand data risk, they treat the story like universal truth. These people are sometimes swayed by fear-based marketing (Hastings et al., 2004); because they don't have a full understanding of the numbers, they don't think critically about the information they receive and they latch on to the fear.

Casual

Casual data users understand a few key bits of data, but not many. They may understand that data is important but not necessarily have skills to use it, or not see the value in data but know they need to start learning.

Your upline who shows a graph in a meeting and fumbles their way through talking about it – confusing themselves in the process because they don't have a deep understanding of what the graph means and are thrown by questions on elements they don't understand – is probably a casual user. This person might have a good handle on their own finances, but don't really do much more with numbers outside this.

People at this level often have many misconceptions about data – from picking up inaccuracies along the way, or because they don't have much formal or structured training. They might occasionally get things wrong or have some fundamental flaws in their understanding. Often people in this group are attempting to learn and build their understanding, so they can move up the ladder of proficiency.

Aware

An *aware* data and evidence user is developing their understanding of what the numbers tell them, and may be trying to integrate this information in their life or work. People in this stage understand why data is important and why they should invest time and effort in upskilling, and they are generally doing so, or attempting to. They might be testing out new ideas and working with data in slightly different ways to how they have before. They might be starting to think about the things that work and are most useful for them. They may prioritise (or try to prioritise) learning in the data sphere, but are acutely aware of the time it takes and the effort required to get them to where they want to be.

Active

When someone is an *active* data user, they are thinking about how the numbers and insights gleaned from the data inform their life or work. People who take action because of a shift in the housing market, or change the exposure of items in a store based on best sellers, are not just having a 'good idea' – they are engaging in evidence-informed decision-making. Not only are people at this level able to read, interpret and understand the numbers, they are able to see how the evidence connects with real people, real contexts and their life. They explore the ways that they might use this information to make things better. People in this category will not always get it right – after all, life is never just as easy as a straight cause-and-effect or input-versus-outputs scenario – but they are giving it a good go.

Reflective

Moving beyond action takes a person to the point of being a *reflective* user. They use data and evidence to inform action, reflect on the impact the action has had, then continue to refine and adjust as they go.

People in this stage realise that there is no 'magic bullet' or perfect solution; but a cycle of ongoing data collection, analysis, action and reflection helps them refine what they do. They might adjust share purchases based on the market, regularly refine organisational goals and actions, or use social media analytics to shape, inform and refine their marketing strategy over time. The reflection stage is innovation, action and research at work. As Simon Sinek said in his book *The Infinite Game* (2019), there is no finish line – reflective data users are infinitely learning, evolving and adjusting.

Moving up the data-use levels

Regardless of where you are on the data-use continuum, you can and will improve your skill and understanding if you try. This book provides you with the tools and knowledge to become more effective in using data to inform your decision-making. As your skill improves, you will move up the levels until you are adept at using data to inform action, and reflect and refine as you go.

While moving up the levels is the goal for anyone who wants to have more impact, it is important to recognise that this growth takes time and effort. Moving from one level to the next requires time, exposure and practice, and requires you to shed some of the preconceived ideas that you have around data and evidence-informed decision-making. However, the greater your use of evidence in your decision-making, the more likely it is that your actions will have a positive impact and you can lead shifts in your own life, with your family and within your organisation.

My passage through the levels occurred while I was working as a secondary school teacher. At the start of my career, I was completely unaware of the impact of data in the classroom and school – I was focused on how I did my job, how I taught the curriculum and how I built relationships with the kids. The idea of data was completely foreign to me, other than marking assignments or exams and giving a letter grade, or a percentage-correct score. I moved up to the level of *conscious* data use when I moved to the United Kingdom, where

I heard regular conversations about data but didn't really understand what it was all about. (I was, to be honest, more concerned with when it was going to stop raining!) I moved up to become a *casual* user as I began to understand some of the key indicators that were tracked and used in schools (such as the percentage of students who passed particular subjects).

After a few months in a middle management role I became an *aware* user, and started to think more about the data that applied to me in my role and my team. It was a steep learning curve, accelerated by the data-driven culture, the high expectations of fast learning and the senior leaders' active development of my skills in support and suggested models. As I learned more, became faster and could understand the data more quickly, I became more able to connect it to my own practice. I tried out some ways of addressing the challenges many of my students faced.

I transitioned to the *active* level when I started trying new things, testing out ideas and talking to my team members about how they were using their data. We set some goals and sought to improve the pass rates in our subjects by collecting and using data for things we could control.

I became a *reflective* user when I started learning from my mistakes, evolving and adapting what I did in my department and in my classroom, and trying to innovate in my teaching strategies and with my team. Sure, we made mistakes; but we were guided by the evidence that we had access to and collected, it informed our decision-making, and it meant that we had a considerable impact on student outcomes. We were able to double the percentage of students who passed my subject in a 12-month period, and most of that was due to the way that we collected and responded to the data. There was a similar percentage point increase in the second year I was in the role.

Although my experience with data started in schools and classrooms, the idea of using and responding to data is far bigger than this context. While the context changes depending on the field you are in, the principles of capitalising on data remain the same – you must put people first; be solutions-oriented in your data use; and remember that when data is not acted upon, it has no impact at all.

Becoming a numbers person

In my work as a data coach and storyteller since I left the classroom, I have learned about the challenges that individuals and organisations face in using evidence to inform their decision-making. Sometimes that comes down to a lack of confidence. It's usually due to limited training or exposure to learning opportunities. Often leaders tell me that they are embarrassed to ask for additional help, as they believe they should already have the skills and understanding of how to use data in their role.

This book aims to help you (and members of your team) move up the levels of data use, so that you can engage with the evidence that you have to make better, evidence-informed decisions in your sphere of influence. That might be in your own work or your small team in your small business, or you might be an executive looking to become more fluent in the use of data.

This book is designed to be read from start to finish if you are new to data, but each of the five chapters offers standalone content that will assist in whichever element of data use you would like to dig into. Chapter 1 considers the question 'why data and why now?' and unpacks some of the ways that you should think about the data that you are given. Chapter 2 focuses on understanding the numbers, and it includes a discussion on different types of data that are available, including quantitative and qualitative data types. This chapter also explores how to decide which data is most important. Chapter 3 covers visualising data – in other words, representing data in a graphical way.

It discusses the way people read visualisations, developing your own visualisations, and knowing how to choose the best visualisation for your aims.

Chapters 4 and 5 focus on the notion of data storytelling, which is the ultimate goal of using data. Chapter 4 looks at establishing trends in data, including some of the fundamental principles you must understand when thinking about data, and possible models of analysis questions you can use in the process. There are plenty of ways that human brains want to work against us with data – including confirmation bias and loss aversion – but if you can recognise these regular patterns and trends, then you can rethink the data and the way you respond to it. Chapter 5 considers how to make decisions, talk about data and work with others to collaboratively establish actions as a result of the information you have.

Each chapter steps you through the elements of data storytelling, to progressively build your skills in the aspects needed to critically engage with the data and to tell effective data stories.

Data storytelling involves thinking about what the numbers tell you about real people and real lives, and considering what your actions should be as a result of knowing that information. You won't effectively engage with and use data unless you get to this point. In saying that, your data literacy and visualisation skills are not fixed, or something that you can tick a box and move on from if you feel you have it handled. In new roles, as time progresses, and as new data sets are introduced, you'll need to go back and learn about the context of the new metrics (or measures) and different types of visualisations, so that you can return to a place of data storytelling with the new information you have. In other words, being an effective data storyteller involves continual engagement and curiosity. Unfortunately, research suggests that only one in 10 organisations engages with data storytelling on a regular basis (Tischler et al., 2017), and that organisations are not investing enough in building employees' data storytelling skills (Amini et al., 2018).

I hope that you find this book engaging, useful and more interesting than the maths textbooks that you used to hate when you were in school. Numbers can be fun – I promise. They can teach you a lot, and they can help you make good decisions. But to use data in this way, you need to replace your fear of numbers with curiosity. You need to know how to read the data and use it effectively. Once you do this, you, too, can become a numbers person.

Chapter 1

Why data literacy?

'But I'm not a numbers person…'

(said by too many people, all the time)

Data is everywhere. Smart watches track our blood oxygen levels. Google Maps predicts the best route to our appointment depending on the day and time that we get into our car. The DRS (umpire decision review system) confirms cricket wicket decisions from the snicko, heat map and ball trajectory estimates. Social media predicts who you might want to connect with and what you want to buy. No matter what industry you work in, or where you live, data is pervasive.

Because our workplaces and organisations are microcosms of broader society, the use and implication of data will continue to evolve and develop in the coming generations, and will keep increasing at an exponential rate. No longer will governments or investors support organisations that can't provide solid evidence of impact, with funding increasingly redirected elsewhere when departments or organisations do not perform.

We have better access to information about our own habits than ever before. My Apple Watch tells me how many days in the last week and month I hit my exercise, movement and standing goals, and my banking app on my phone sorts my spending into 'buckets' so I can see how much I spent on eating out (too much), education (too much) and technology subscriptions (don't care – worth it!).

In small business, numbers help us make decisions. When I floated the idea of this book with my publisher, I outlined my intended market and the aims of the book, and provided chapter summaries. Yet the first conversation we had started with the numbers: required investment costs, royalty rates, which comparable books have sold how many copies and so on. In the corporate world, success often depends on the numbers – whether that be clients won, billable hours or on-time performance. But it isn't just the big performance indicators that matter; it's the nitty gritty, smaller data points along the way that you must be able to read, unpack and question at the appropriate time.

In some ways, this makes sense. Why would my book publisher invest in editorial, design and marketing if the data shows that books on this topic don't sell? It would be a crazy decision, leading to money lost due to pursuing a project the data indicated was a poor choice. Why would investors continue to invest in organisations that are underperforming? Why would business owners persist if the data indicates the market and clients are not responding to their products or services?

However, using evidence to inform decision-making can be tricky – particularly if you are new to business, don't have experience using or acting on data or don't have the tools and resources you need. Often, regardless of the size of your organisation, the issue isn't that you *don't* have the data – it's that you don't necessarily know what to do with it. In a 2018 Gartner survey of chief data officers' views on roadblocks to success, 'poor data literacy' was the second-highest-ranked roadblock, behind 'culture challenges to accept change', and just ahead of 'lack of relevant skills or staff'.

One of the reasons many people struggle to effectively put data to work is the time it takes from collecting the data to acting on it. Some industry research indicates that, in working with data, approximately 80 per cent of the time is taken up collecting and organising the data to ensure it is in a format that is useable, meaning that only 20 per cent of the time is spent on putting the data to work (Jones & Pickett, 2019). Even though the final 20 percent of effort is the most important, and is the part that will have an impact, often people tire or stop once the organisation or visualisation of the data is done. Sometimes, the organisation process takes so long that people have run out of steam, become distracted by the next challenge or been pulled away to focus on fixing another problem, so they don't get to the final part – actually using the data. At home and in the workplace, we need to focus on putting the data we're collecting and organising to work. We need to spend more time considering the ways evidence can be used to support our decision-making. As leaders, we also need to actively minimise the 80 per cent – whether that be through technical solutions or automating the process as much as possible – so we can get our best people working on the 20 per cent, but also increase that proportion to focus on solutions.

Data-informed versus data-driven

When talking about the ways in which data can be used, there is an important distinction to be made between being data-informed (which is what we want to be) and being data-driven (what we do not want to be). Being data-driven is like a horse wearing blinkers in a horse race – they can see the finish line and the goal, but they can't see what is going on either side of them. They race towards the finish line, with minimal distractions, and a limited understanding of what other horses and riders are doing. Data-driven organisations are ruthless around the numbers. They move staff on if they don't meet targets; they change their product lines to increase market share; and they callously make all the big decisions based on what the numbers suggest will work. I do not believe that organisations should aspire to be data-driven, because despite the fact that I am a numbers person, the data (particularly if you're relying on one piece of quantitative data) can never tell you the whole picture.

Conversely, being data-informed is like being a racehorse without blinkers. They can see the goal and the finish line and they know what they are aiming for, but they can also take in the speed of horses around them, their position relative to others and slight shifts in movement from horses on all sides of them. There is a finish line, they are working towards it, but they are aware of the context they're in. Being data-informed in business is much the same. When you're data-informed, you use the numbers and rely on them to provide information about where you are going and what you need to do to improve, but you also incorporate your understanding of context, people, the financial climate, market demand and company culture into the decision-making process. When you are data-informed, you don't make decisions driven by the data – you make decisions that are *informed* and *influenced* by the data. Organisations should always aspire to be data-informed if they want to effectively harness the power of data, but never be driven by it.

The aftermath of the September 11 United States terrorist attack is a tragic example of data-driven decision-making gone wrong. Ken Feinberg's book *What is Life Worth? The unprecedented effort to compensate the victims of 9/11* (2006) and the subsequent film *Worth*, directed by Sara Colangelo (2020), both document Feinberg's work as the US Government's Special Master of the September 11th Victim Compensation Fund. This fund had the enormous challenge of compensating thousands of families for their losses due to the attacks. It was tasked with coming up with a dollar figure for each life lost, taking into consideration income, age and marital status. Feinberg's team's initial approach was data-driven, as essentially there was a formula, where demographic details were entered to develop a payout figure for each person. The victims' families quickly realised that this algorithm led to significant disparities in payout figures. They were angry. People questioned why their relative was not 'worth' as much as others; it was heartbreaking. Over time, as Feinberg met more families and heard their stories, his approach changed. He learned of different contexts with partners and children, and he attempted to find solutions for longer-term illnesses beyond the two-year program. Ever so slowly, Feinberg and his team modified the fund, built trust with families and achieved the threshold amount of families signing up for the fund. In the end, the fund was responsible for more than 5000 families receiving over US$7 billion in compensation. Although it was, in many ways, an impossible task, the initial data-driven approach was never going to work.

Amazon founder Jeff Bezos is a successful business leader who is data-informed rather than data-driven. This might come as a surprise, as many people assume that Bezos is, in fact, data-driven. However, Bezos once said:

> 'People think of Amazon as very data-oriented and I always tell them, look, if you can make the decision with data, make the decision with data… But a lot of the most important decisions simply cannot be made with data.'
>
> (Mejia, 2018)

Bezos advocates for a combination of data and gut to inform decision-making, rather than being driven solely by the data, and he is very comfortable talking about the importance of being data-informed. Take for example the launch of Amazon Prime. Bezos reported that the numbers indicated that Amazon Prime *would not* be successful. If he had considered the numbers only, he would not have pursued what is now a key element of Amazon's success. Despite the numbers indicating it might not work, Bezos understood the broader context and emerging market around the idea and decided to go with his gut, despite what the data was telling him. Bezos said, 'you collect as much data as you can. You immerse yourself in that data… but then make the decision with your heart' (Mejia, 2018).

What is data?

In the preceding pages I have deliberately used the terms 'data' and 'evidence' interchangeably. That is because I see them as one and the same. For me, data is not limited to the quantitative numerical information that we so often see – for example, when we are shown share market figures at the end of the news each night. It also includes 'data' that is qualitative, observational and self-reported. While numbers are often easier to measure, track and visualise, the additional qualitative evidence and data types that sit alongside the numbers provide rich context and detail about their meaning.

Continuing with the metaphor of the news, we consume plenty of 'data' daily that is not in the form of numbers. A crime report might discuss crime rates, or show graphs or maps of the prevalence of crime (which is quantitative and visually represented), but we also develop our understanding of the facts through the narrative told, the language used, the expressions on the faces of victims and newsreaders, and through photos and voice and video recordings.

The combination of different data sources builds our understanding of crime in our local area, and ensures that we have a much more comprehensive understanding of the situation than if we were only presented with graphs or numbers.

In saying that, different news broadcasters will report the facts differently or highlight different data – whether this be due to financial backers, owners, governance, geographical location or political persuasion. A news report on two different news channels might be based on the same fundamental information, but the interpretation and delivery of the data differs. In the United States, take for example *The Wall Street Journal*, which has been published since 1889 and is considered a 'newspaper of record'. *The Wall Street Journal* presents information differently to, say, Fox News, which was started by Rupert Murdoch to cater for more conservative viewers. It doesn't really matter which news source you prefer – what is important is to recognise that they are different. They have different priorities and goals, and consequently they can report the same story in different ways. They choose different facts to highlight; they use more or less emotive or persuasive language; they include different images, videos and parts of the story. In other words, they select the data (qualitative or quantitative) that will help them tell the story in the way they want to tell it.

The website GapMinder is a good example of this process of selecting and combining multiple types of information to develop a narrative (Harford, 2020). In its pursuit of eradicating global misconceptions, GapMinder uses statistics to address misunderstandings about factors such as poverty, gender inequality, global warming and refugees. Its 'Dollar Street' tool takes the notion of a numerical monthly income, which is quite abstract and difficult to understand, and adds a visual to demonstrate what that reality looks like for people around the world. Dollar Street includes thousands of photos that show the difference between the types and condition of shoes that different people own, where they go to the toilet, what their front door looks like and what their hands look like. It is a powerful tool that brings the human story to the wealth gap, which is sometimes difficult to truly understand if we are given numbers alone. It is a great example of the power of numbers and visuals working together to make meaning. When you can build a narrative around the numbers, people are far more likely to remember them – and you'll have a greater impact.

Data democracy

The exponential increase in the amount of data we have will cause shifts in the access we have to data – not only as consumers in our personal lives, but increasingly in our workplaces. Organisations, and the world more generally, are moving into what Qlik – the Fortune 500's official analytics partner – calls the third generation of business intelligence: a data democracy (Qlik, 2019). Your organisation might already be there, you might be a long way away, but the reality is that we are all heading in this direction.

The first generation of business intelligence was centralised. Data was generally held and analysed by a small group of staff, usually in the IT department. Very few people had direct access to data at this stage, and Qlik estimates that, at best, business analytics were reaching a maximum of 25 per cent of the workforce (Qlik, 2019). The way that this 25 per cent accessed the information was most commonly through formulating a question for the analytics team, and the analyst would go away, crunch the numbers, and provide the response to the question with a simple answer or report (Qlik, 2019). This centralised model was limited in effectiveness because nobody besides the analysts was required to have data skills, which meant that others in the organisation were not able to explore the data – they had to ask quite closed questions and, in return, they received quite closed answers.

In the second generation of business intelligence, data was decentralised. It became accessible to more employees, and more people were able to interact with data for the first time (Qlik, 2019). This stage included technical solutions that allowed a greater number of employees to explore the trends, and ask questions of the data themselves – rather than the ask-wait-answer model of the first generation. In this stage, data sets were often held in multiple places by multiple people; consequently, storage solutions were untidy. Data literacy across the whole organisation became a glaring challenge, as more people could see the data but did not necessarily know what to do with it (or how to do it).

The third generation of business intelligence – data democracy – is where more staff have skills and access to the data, and augmented analytics is used to understand trends and meaning in the data (Qlik, 2019). All employees can access the data they need, when they need it, and it is used in a responsible manner. Data is not seen as the destination but part of the journey, where it is embedded in daily decision-making and is a part of organisational culture. Some organisations are at this point now, but many are not.

There are two parts of the data democracy that are particularly important:

1. Building user skills so people can use and act on the data they have access to
2. Embedding organisational structures, expectations and support to create a culture of collaboration.

Both of these need to happen together. If you make data available to people who don't know how to use it, quite simply, they won't. If you build people's skills but they can't access the data, they will wonder why you trained them, and become frustrated at the lack of information that they have available.

Some leaders fear what might happen if they make data freely available. What if someone mishandles the data or shares something they find with someone they shouldn't? This is a legitimate concern. In an organisation where sharing and democratising data is new, there is certainly a need to think this process through – to plan out the rollout, and ensure that you include necessary training for staff. An organisation I worked with recently created a data security and safety module that all employees completed – this was a way of communicating a consistent message to employees about appropriate versus inappropriate use of data. It also clearly connected any misuse of data to disciplinary action, in the same way that other breaches of codes of conduct would. Be very clear about your expectations, train your staff and follow through when you need to. But do not let the fear hold you back.

The biggest challenge, however, that I experience when I work with organisations is the siloed or detached systems that operate in many companies – where separate data is held by individual teams, rather than being shared across the organisation. I recently worked with a company that had a team of around 15 advertising staff and 35 sales staff. The advertising team had a host of useful information – such as the click rates on online ads, the reach of different advertising campaigns, and geographical information about areas that had greater advertisement engagement than others. The sales team had brilliant information on things like the regions with the largest sales, sales figures by postcode, average spend per customer, and customers who had potential purchases sitting in carts online. Both teams had great sets of information, which undoubtedly assisted them in doing their respective jobs. But these two teams did not have access to one another's data! The advertising team couldn't see the sales figures, and the sales team couldn't see who the advertising was targeting.

Just because one team collects a specific set of data does not mean that they are the only team that could find the information useful or beneficial in their work (Hamilton, 2017). While there are many obstacles to overcome in getting data to work for you, and monetising it – such as quality, standardisation and security (Ismail, 2019) – organisational structures that limit the way data is shared is a recurring theme. As Jay Cline from PwC reportedly said:

> '31 per cent [of organisations] said we are organisationally siloed – the data that belongs to one business unit is locked up in that business unit, it is not shared with other business units – so they're not getting the full value of their data, just because of the structure.'
>
> (In Ismail, 2019)

When data is locked away, and held exclusively by a group or a team, organisations can't possibly capitalise on its benefits or put the data to work. Working in silos limits data's power and impact. The solution is to actively work to break down the silos, promote a data democracy in our teams and across our organisations, and allow people the opportunity to work with the data that maximises the impact they can have in their work.

Data misuse

While websites such as GapMinder and Dollar Street highlight the ways that multiple types of data can convey a message, it is worth mentioning that sometimes data is misused. Manipulation or misuse of information to prove a point is one of the main criticisms of data that I hear in my work. It's the reason some people turn away from data.

It is, of course, possible to select data that tells you what you want to hear or say, or omit data that does not align with your goals. It's also possible to manipulate a graph's axis to make sales, growth or company reach look better or worse – depending on what you want to prove. However, this reality does not negate the utility or power of data. If anything, it emphasises the importance of developing data-literate citizens who can critically review, understand and question the data they have been given.

As a former Year 9 maths teacher, I spent many years teaching teenagers how to read data critically and identify times that data had been used or presented in a way that was manipulative. I would show my students a range of visualisations shared in the media and we would talk about how the chosen visualisation was used to make the point, and we would manipulate the graph to show a different story.

A common task I ran in this unit was to survey students about whether they preferred to drink Coca-Cola or Pepsi. I would collect the class data and graph it, but I would deliberately do it twice, for two different audiences. If 12 people told me that they preferred Coca-Cola, and 11 told me they preferred Pepsi, I could manipulate the graph (as shown in figure 1.1) to make it appear that there was not much difference in preference. I would talk with my students about how, if I was trying to prove that Pepsi was almost as popular as Coke, I would choose to use this view.

However, if I worked for Coca-Cola, and wanted to highlight the gap and make it appear as though many more young people enjoyed Coke than Pepsi, all I would need to do is manipulate the axis values to make the gap appear larger (shown in figure 1.2). Both graphs contain the same data and are essentially the same graphical representation of the data; the only thing that is different is the vertical axis (y-axis).

However, the difference between the two, and the associated meaning (if you don't have the skills to discern the issue with the second graph), is incredibly obvious.

Figure 1.1: Graph manipulated to show little preference between drinks

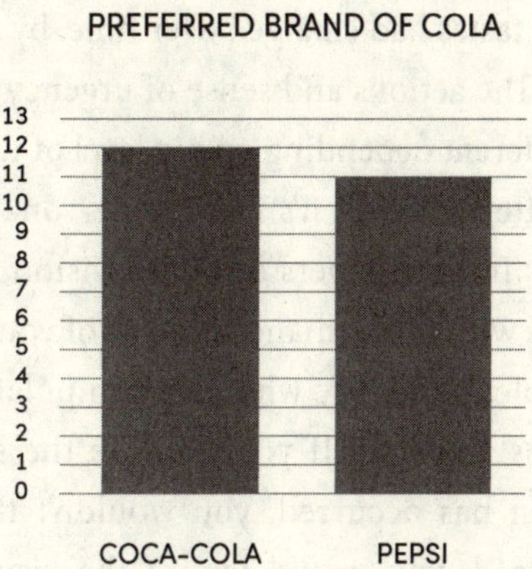

Figure 1.2: Graph manipulated to show larger gap in preferences

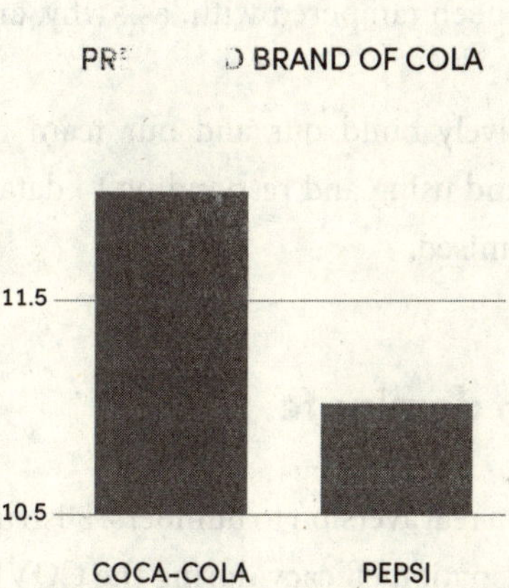

Graph manipulation is particularly problematic when the consumer is unaware of the manipulation. If I worked for Pepsi and saw figure 1.2 but didn't pay attention to the vertical axis, I would be rallying my troops, thinking about what we are doing wrong, and potentially investing time and effort into bridging the gap between us and the other company. However, if I were aware of data manipulation and how to read graphs, I would not be alarmed. Instead, I would probably question whether tastes had changed over time, by seeking other data to compare it to. The actions and sense of urgency around a solution would be very different depending on my level of understanding.

It doesn't matter whether it's in your personal life, and you are looking at graphs in newspapers or on television, or at work, when you are presented with performance reports of your team – you need the skills to be able to identify whether manipulation is happening, and question it as required. If you do have the skills to recognise that manipulation has occurred, you wouldn't then disregard the data itself – instead, you would ignore the visualisation and the associated storytelling. Asking for or creating a new visualisation would be a good place to start. In this instance, starting the y-axis at a value of 0, and keeping the increments the same throughout, is a good way to address the issues. If you are looking at a graph and can see the axes have been tampered with, ask why, and ask for another visualisation.

As we collectively build our and our team members' skills in critical thinking and using and responding to data, concerns such as these will be minimised.

How fear can dominate

Some people have a real aversion to numbers. Distrust in governments, numbers and vaccination efficacy during the COVID-19 pandemic is a significant global example of this. Regardless of your personal views, many of the statistics and information provided via the media have been regularly and repeatedly scrutinised, pulled apart and questioned. While it is important to think critically about the information that we are presented, and ask questions when we do not know the answers, there have been many instances of unjustified distrust – for example, people without a medical or science background doubting medical professionals and the science.

Beyond the scepticism throughout the pandemic, there are, more generally, large numbers of our population who fear data and numbers. For many, this stems all the way back to their experience with maths in school, particularly as they moved into secondary school (Dowker et al., 2016). Many refer to this phenomenon as 'maths anxiety' – and it's not a new phenomenon. Back in 1972, Richardson and Suinn defined maths anxiety as 'a feeling of tension and anxiety that interferes with the manipulation of numbers and the solving of mathematical problems in... ordinary life and academic situations'. While different studies of maths anxiety have found different rates of maths anxiety in the population, the review of studies by Dowker et al. in 2016 reported that it affects anywhere between 2 and 30 per cent of the population. Even if the very lowest rate (2 per cent) were accurate, that would mean that 158 million people globally are affected by the challenge of using and manipulating numbers.

Negativity bias is another factor that contributes to people's fear of numbers. Despite all of the good things that happen to us, negativity bias means that we tend to focus on the thing that didn't go well, discounting the tens, or hundreds, of things that did go well. Researchers Rozin and Royzman (2001) use an age-old Russian adage to describe the power of negativity bias: 'A spoonful of tar can spoil a barrel of honey, but a spoonful of honey does nothing for a barrel of tar.' In other words, the smallest amount of negativity can spoil a whole barrel of happiness, while a small amount of happiness does nothing to a barrel of negativity.

About five years prior to writing this book I undertook a 360-degree review of my performance. I completed a self-evaluation, a senior leader completed a review of my work, and people I worked with every day completed a review. For each criterion in the tool I received three scores – mine, my leader's, and the aggregate score of all the other responses. Despite the review being largely positive, and there generally being alignment between my perception of my strengths and weaknesses and others' perceptions, I focused on the negatives. In fact, not only did I focus on the negatives, I could not let them go. I fixated on who said what, and on why they gave me low scores, but spent very little time thinking about the positives. That's negativity bias for you!

Negativity bias can affect our view of the numbers in different ways. The first is that we tend to assume data will only highlight the things that are going wrong. We are worried that the data will reveal that we haven't been doing something well, and then others will start asking questions about us and our performance. I worked with a senior leader recently who did not have a good understanding about the data, and when I dug deeper, I uncovered that he was petrified of what the results would say about his leadership. However, rather than learning and embracing the numbers (and attempting to lead positive change), he put his head in the sand and tried to ignore them. This had worked well for him in the past, but when his board started pushing him on the numbers, he was suddenly in the spotlight and having to upskill quickly, *and* justify trends that he had not seen or acted upon.

The second way that negativity bias affects us is that when we are engaging with data, we focus on the negatives. Rather than being objective and impartial, seeing the positives and the negatives equally, negativity bias draws our attention to negative trends. Negative data always exists – there will always be approaches or meetings that do not convert to sales, routes that do not perform on time, or cases that we could not win. None of us is perfect, and therefore the data will never paint a perfect picture of us. But we need to ensure that we take the good with the bad and avoid focusing on the negatives disproportionately to the positives.

I recently worked with an executive leader who sent me his annual summary data for his 10 key performance indicators (KPIs). His strategic goal was to improve each metric every year; however, in the 12-month period, his organisation improved in six areas, and dropped slightly in four. He reached out to me and said, 'I'm planning on putting a rocket up my staff tomorrow morning about this. Can you please just check I haven't missed anything?' I'm so glad he reached out to me. When I spoke to him, I flipped his initial analysis on its head. I highlighted the six areas of improvement (and the considerable percentage improvement for each). We talked through the four areas that were lower, and the fact that they were lower by less than one percentage point each. We discussed statistical significance and the fact that, yes, the numbers in those metrics were not higher than the prior year, but in reality, they weren't too different. None of the KPIs showed a significant drop or flagged a concern for me. As a result of our conversation, he completely changed tack for the staff meeting the next day. I encouraged him to focus on celebration first, then a discussion about how they could move the other indicators forward. I am glad he took a moment to seek a second set of eyes and a different perspective on the data, because who knows how much damage his negativity bias might have done to his team if he had proceeded as planned.

Evidence versus action

Data and evidence should be used in a way that is solutions-oriented and informs action. Despite the fear that may dominate, it's important to realise there is so much potential in the numbers. Data can tell you so much about your work and your organisation – but you have to be actually *using* it to capitalise on this potential.

People generally fit into one of four categories in terms of taking action as a result of the information they have access to (as shown in figure 1.3): stasis, guess work, lost opportunity or impact.

Figure 1.3: Four categories of evidence versus action

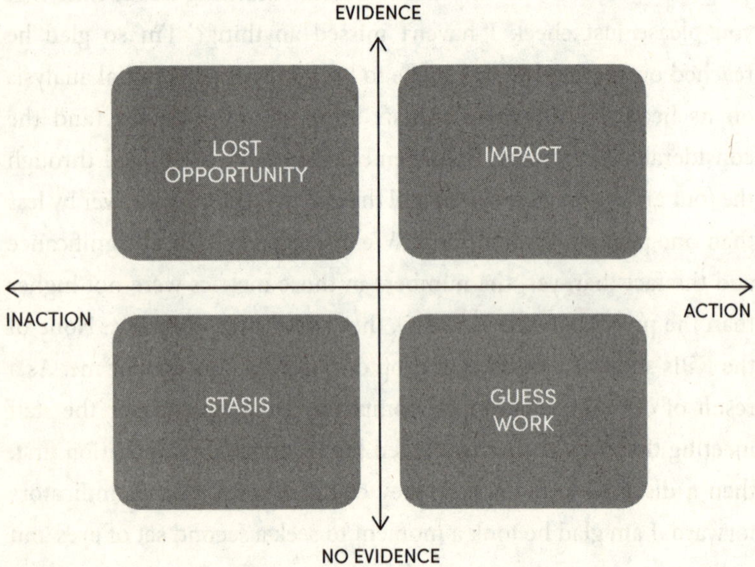

The challenge is not only in identifying where you and your team members sit, but in thinking about how you move into the goal quadrant: impact.

A small number of people fit into the *stasis* category. People in this quadrant don't tap into the data or evidence that is available to them, and they take limited action. They're hesitant to change their approach. People in *stasis* generally do the same thing they have always done and are happy to continue doing so, even though it might not be the most efficient or impactful way of doing things. People like this might leave their savings in their transaction account rather than an offset account where they could reduce their expenses, because that is what they have always done. In business, they're leaders and colleagues who say, 'This has worked for me for years, so I'm going to keep doing it this way.' This is not a productive way of thinking, because the world around us is constantly changing – as are we, and our organisations. Being in this state of *stasis* is not particularly helpful for our loved ones, our colleagues, our teams, or the enterprise of which we are a part.

Some people sit in the quadrant of *guess work*. People in this category are keen to make changes, to try new ways of doing things, but they do not necessarily use or rely on the evidence they have to inform their decisions. These are the people in our lives who jump from one job or relationship to the next, always chasing the 'next best thing' – and they may have been burned by poor or rash decisions in the past. In this quadrant are companies that expand too quickly out of greed or desire for market share, but that have not done any homework on what the market needs. I feel for people in this category, because they want more and try to do more, but they don't use the evidence available to them to help shape or guide the changes they make.

There are two reasons people in this category don't harness the data or evidence available in their decision-making:

- They can't make sense of the data they have, in that they may not have the skills to identify what is important, know how to read it, or understand how it can inform their decisions.

- They do not believe in or trust the evidence, so they deliberately disregard it.

Either way, people in the state of *guess work* are missing a huge opportunity to reflect on what they already know and the feedback they have access to, and are always in a process of 'trial and error'.

In my work with leaders and organisations, I have found that most people sit in the quadrant of *lost opportunity*. People in this category have access to the evidence but are taking no action. I see this happening in many organisations. I am yet to be asked to help an organisation 'find more data' – it is more common that I work with people to put the data they already have to use, or to direct their attention to the most important metrics for them.

Organisations and employees may be in this quadrant for a few reasons:

- They have too much data and don't know what they should pay attention to or how to use it, so they choose not to use it.
- They're surrounded by data but don't use it because they don't have the skills to engage with it.
- They have access to a lot of data but deliberately avoid seeking out the insights because they lack trust in the numbers.
- They're unsure how the trends they notice can be used to shift what they do.
- They're fearful of leading change and worry about getting it wrong.

If you don't act on the information that is available to you, it is a lost opportunity. Our organisations and lives are filled with data that we could be harnessing to shape our decisions, but many people are missing out on capitalising on this information.

The goal is to get to the quadrant of *impact*. This is where individuals, teams and organisations have access to data; they use the evidence that is available to them; and they make decisions and take action as a result. People in this category are trying new things. Many are aware that things will not always go to plan, but trying something is better than staying the same. Even if their evidence-informed change doesn't always pay off, people in the impact category are still positively impacting families and workplaces because they are trying things, learning from their mistakes and adjusting accordingly. They realise that the chance that something may not be successful is not a reason to avoid trying.

If you believe that you, a family member, a colleague, your team or your organisation is in a quadrant other than *impact*, it is worth thinking about how you can move out of that quadrant and towards the upper right-hand corner. Like moving up the ladder of proficiency with using data, the useful reflection to engage in is how you might move from one to the next.

If you are in the *stasis* quadrant, your next step would be to move into the *lost opportunity* quadrant or the *guess work* quadrant before setting your sights on the impact quadrant. You can't go from having no evidence and taking no action to instantly having evidence and taking action. The best path through to impact is via the *lost opportunity* stage – rather than jumping straight to action (the *guess work* quadrant) before you thoroughly understand the data. Don't start taking action yet, but begin to learn about the information that you have access to. Learn about the different measures, what they mean and what additional information you can access, and begin to critically think about the utility of different types of information in your sphere of influence. By developing your understanding of what is going on around you and the information you have access to, you can explore the ways that this information might be useful to guide decision-making in the future.

If you are in the *guess work* quadrant, your goal is to move into the *impact* quadrant by increasing the evidence that you access and use to inform your decisions. It might be that you do more research into the different metrics that your organisation has available. You might seek to develop your understanding of the trends, and think about the ways that this information might shape what you do. You might also attempt to slow down the action and changes while you consult with the evidence. When trying to use more evidence in your decision-making, also consider what the research or literature says – not only about your own specific situation, but about the types of decisions, actions and changes that have been shown to have significant impact in other, similar situations in the past. Not only will you use evidence from within your organisation – that is, the information you collect directly – but also what case studies and other research tells you about the market, the economy and leading change.

In this chapter we've explored the idea of data and evidence in our world today, and considered the way that organisations and individuals are evolving in the prevalence and use of data. When making decisions and drawing on the evidence to guide these shifts in what we do, we all fit into one of four categories: stasis, guess work, lost opportunity or impact. Knowing where we are and how much our decisions are influenced by evidence allows us to identify ways to move towards making better decisions that positively impact our world. In saying that, there are ways that we can think about data that will ultimately impact the way we see, view and analyse it. By being aware of the factors that seek to work against us, we can be better equipped to engage in critical and rigorous data-informed conversations.

Key points

- Seek to be data-informed rather than data-driven. Data-informed is where you look at the numbers but also use your understanding of context, people, teams and so on to guide your decision-making.
- 'Data' or 'evidence' does not have to be quantitative. It covers any type of information that provides a deeper understanding about what you are investigating.
- Organisations are moving towards being in the third generation of business intelligence, which is where data is democratised for employees.
- In a data democracy, data is made available to employees in a responsible manner, so it is accessible when they need it.
- Data misuse is when people manipulate data to deliberately deceive the consumer. By understanding the ways this can occur, you are more readily able to recognise and question it.
- Richardson and Suinn defined maths anxiety as 'a feeling of tension and anxiety that interferes with the manipulation of numbers and the solving of mathematical problems in… ordinary life and academic situations' (1972).
- Despite all of the good things that happen to us, negativity bias means that we tend to focus on the thing that didn't go well, discounting the tens, or hundreds, of things that did go well.
- Generally, people fit into one of four categories when it comes to using evidence and taking action: stasis, guess work, lost opportunity or impact.

Reflection questions

- Do you think you are more data-informed or data-driven? What language do you use that reaffirms this position? If you are more data-driven, how can you seek to be more data-informed?
- When you think of 'data' and 'evidence', what do you think of?
- What types of data and evidence do you regularly use?
- What other types of information do you have access to?
- Where is your organisation in the three generations of business intelligence?
- What are your thoughts on a data democracy?
- In what ways do you see the idea of a data democracy being relevant to your work context?
- What challenges does your organisation face in building a data democracy?
- Do you have any concerns about data misuse in your sphere of influence? If so, how do you go about reducing and removing this challenge?
- Do you suffer from maths anxiety? Or do you know someone who does? If so, what strategies or next steps could you take to reduce the impact?
- When is a time that you have witnessed the impact of negativity bias? If you see it in the future, what are some things that you might be able to say to minimise the focus on the negatives?
- Which quadrant are you in on the evidence versus action model? Why would you put yourself in that quadrant?

- If you are not in the *impact* quadrant, how can you move from where you are towards this point?
- Which quadrant are your team members/colleagues in on the evidence versus action model? If they are not in the *impact* quadrant, what can you do to support them to move towards this point?

Chapter 2

Understanding numbers

> 'All data is a shadow of what has flowed before. Data is reality distilled with intention. We no longer have to picture data as an impenetrable monolith. When we think about data, we should consider the world that delivered it to us.'
>
> (Andrews, 2019)

From the work I have done in a range of organisations over the last decade and a half, I clearly see that there are three key areas to tackle to use data effectively (see figure 2.1 overleaf). The first is data literacy (understanding the numbers); the second is data visualisation (putting it into graphs, tables and other visuals); and the third is data storytelling (establishing what the data is telling you, and responding to it). The ultimate goal of effective data use is to get to the point of data storytelling, but you first need to ensure that you have a solid foundation of data literacy and have access to visualisations that support your analysis.

The journey through these three stages is not necessarily one-way or linear. You might develop (or have) good data literacy skills, develop (or have) great visualisations and engage in effective storytelling, but over time, metrics change, jobs change and you change who you work for. For these reasons, you need to be flexible and adaptable, and happy to jump back and learn about new numbers or new visualisations if and when you need to.

Figure 2.1: Three key elements of effective data use

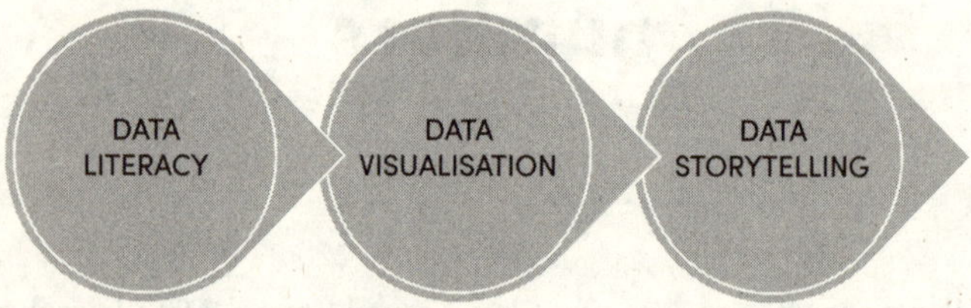

Jim Collins – author of *Good to Great: Why some companies make the leap… and others don't* (2001) – and his research team have collected data from more than 1000 Fortune 500 companies to determine how some companies make it from being a 'good' performer to a 'great' performer. He said:

> 'We found no evidence that the good-to-great companies had more or better information than the comparison companies. None. Both sets of companies had virtually identical access to good information. The key, then, lies not in better information, but in turning information into information that cannot be ignored.'

Jim Collins didn't use the word 'storytelling', but his findings speak to this notion. We have enough information in our organisations already, and probably similar information to other organisations... but we need to understand the numbers and be able to convert them into insights in a way that is meaningful and leads to action.

Learning about data is not easy. It's especially tricky if you have limited time and space to do so in your role, or if there are expectations that you already understand the data. The ever-changing nature of organisations, technology and data adds another level of complexity. The idea of learning this whole new beast might be daunting to you, but at this point I would like to point out that it is okay to be unsure and nervous about it. This feeling of discomfort at learning new things and embracing the unknown has been called the 'learning pit' – a term that was largely popularised by James Nottingham (2017). While his learning pit model was initially developed for student learning, it is applicable to adult learning too.

Nottingham said that all learners travel through the learning pit when learning a new skill or developing a new understanding. In doing so, learners have to step outside their comfort zone and into the pit. He noted that learning is a struggle, and the notion of a pit normalises the feeling of overwhelm, bombardment with new information and confusion that we all feel when we are learning.

The first stage of the learning pit is the steep drop off the edge – from initially thinking you have some understanding of the concept, to realising that you may not know as much as you initially thought. That takes you to the bottom of the pit to a point of confusion, as you try to reconcile your previous understanding with the new information that you are provided with. To continue progressing through the pit and to eventually get out, you realise that you need to invest time and effort into the development of the skill or understanding to improve. You start to slowly make your way out of the pit as you start to build connections and learn. You finally make it out of the learning pit when you have faced the challenge, found it hard, persisted and learned, and have a newly acquired skill or understanding.

Take this opportunity to think about which stage of the learning pit you are in, in terms of your understanding of numbers. Are you sliding in, at the initial point of confusion? Or are you trying to work your way out? What about members of your team? In my work facilitating workshops on data storytelling, I see and work with people at all stages of the learning pit – and I usually see all stages in some way in the same day! Sometimes there are people who think they have a good understanding and do not push themselves out of their comfort zone, so they are 'safely' (yet less skilled) out of the pit – but need to go through it to progress. I've seen countless looks of confusion and overwhelm, as people realise there is perhaps more to the use of data than they initially thought. Yet I love seeing the determination on people's faces as they make a resolution with themselves to learn and grow and know more about data storytelling. It is incredibly satisfying to see them build connections, identify structures and models that work for them and associate the new learning with their own team or work environment. When they can do this, I know they are truly out of the pit. This point of satisfaction and achievement is what you should be aspiring to – not only for yourself but for others that you work with.

Data literacy is the first and fundamental step in the data journey. You must understand the data that you have access to in your organisation, team or workplace, and what it does and does not tell you. In your role, you will have access to a range of metrics that are useful and worthy of your attention – for example, staff retention rates, quarterly sales, quarterly profit, profit margins, percentage growth or decline in sales, sales trends, marketing costs, the portion of clients that pay for different services that you offer, where your customers come from... The list really is endless! If you are data literate, you will be able to explain what these different metrics mean, and identify what is important, what is not as important and, ultimately, what you need to track and monitor.

Data literacy is about more than just the numbers themselves – it is also about understanding the broader context that sits around the numbers so you grasp their relevance. In his book *Proofiness: You're being fooled by the numbers* (2010), Charles Seife said:

> '... numbers are interesting only when they give us information about the world. A number only takes on any significance in everyday life when it tells us how many pounds we've gained since last month or how many dollars it will cost to buy a sandwich or how many weeks are left before our taxes are due...'

The context that sits around the numbers helps you attribute meaning to the number itself. You need to be able to understand percentages, but you also need to know that profit margin is different to gross margin and the percentage of returning customers. It is this context that helps you relate the numbers to the real world, and when the numbers become actionable.

As I mentioned in chapter 1, 'data' and therefore 'data literacy' incorporates all the numbers and quantitative information that you have access to, but it also includes the other descriptive, text, artefact, anecdotal and qualitative information that you have as well. These broad categories of data – quantitative and qualitative – have strengths and limitations. One is not better than the other. Both are equally important in every organisation and in data storytelling. For this reason, this chapter will dig into the differences between qualitative and quantitative data and highlight the ways in which these data types can be useful.

Quantitative data

When people talk about the data available in an organisation, they are often referring to quantitative data, which is generally numerical information. Numerical data is incredibly useful. It provides an objective snapshot of what you're investigating; you can quickly see summary statistics such as averages and trends over time; and you can use the numbers to build visualisations relatively easily.

All quantitative data fits into one of two sub-categories: discrete or continuous data. Generally speaking, discrete data is data that fits into broad categories or whole numbers, such as the number of employees you have, the number of products available for sale on your website or the number of active advertising campaigns you have running. In a way, discrete data 'jumps' levels that are generally whole numbers, in that you can't have half a sale, or a board of 5.6 directors. Continuous data is numerical data that can take on decimals. Information such as profit margin or percentage growth can take on any result – not just whole numbers – therefore they are continuous data. Like your height and your weight, these measures do not jump from one measure or whole number (centimetre or kilogram) to the next.

A benefit of quantitative data is that it is relatively easy to collect. You can survey staff or customers on their satisfaction with the organisation or products on a one to five scale; you can see whether this result differs between stakeholders; and you can see whether the results have improved from the previous time you asked the question. A downside of quantitative data is that you often have so much of it – it's difficult to know what exactly you need and what is useful. In addition, each of the different metrics you have (such as profit, percentage growth, customer satisfaction ratings and so on) carry with them a different data literacy requirement. The context and understanding, like in the Charles Seife quote I shared previously, differs for each value. However, in many instances, you have not been shown how to work with the numbers and how to unpack their context and meaning, which makes your ability to discern what is important that bit harder. There are also the added complications of new metrics being added over time; changing roles in our organisation meaning other data becomes more important; or moving to a different organisation that uses different data.

Depending on the type of business that you find yourself working in, the quantitative data you have access to will differ from organisations in other fields. There may be some overlap in some areas, but generally the data profile changes for different industries. People who do the same role as you in a different organisation might focus or rely on different data sets as well. And to add further insult to injury, different teams and individuals in your organisation will use and prioritise different types of data to what you do. No wonder this is not straightforward!

Correlation versus causation

When you're using quantitative data – particularly if you're comparing or measuring one result against another – you must understand the difference between correlation and causation. Correlation is 'a statistical measure that expresses the extent to which two variables are linearly related (meaning they change together at a constant rate)' (SAS Institute Inc, n.d.a.). Essentially, correlation is a measure of the strength of the relationship between two factors, or a measure of whether one thing behaves in a similar manner to something else – but just because two things behave in a similar way does not necessarily mean that one causes the other.

There are plenty of examples of correlation that have nothing to do with causation, including the number of Nicolas Cage movies in a year versus pool drownings, per capita consumption of chicken and total US crude oil imports, the number of marriages in New York City and the number of murders by blunt objects, and Apple iPhone sales and the number of people who die by falling down the stairs (Vigen, n.d.). While these are interesting (and some are amusing), essentially, they are 'correlated' because their graphs move in similar ways over the same time period. Generally, correlation is modelled on a scatterplot, where the independent variable is on the horizontal x-axis and the dependent variable is on the vertical y-axis (more on that in the next chapter).

Causation, on the other hand, is when one thing is deemed to cause the other. We know that the number of Nicolas Cage movies does not *cause* more people to drown in pools – imagine if Cage didn't act for a year, and nobody would drown! Often people jump to quick 'this caused that' assumptions when working with quantitative data, which can be problematic. It takes time and rigorous investigation and research to determine a cause. It is not as simple as looking at two data sets and seeing that they are correlated.

For example, proven causations include that sedentary lifestyles cause heart disease, and that flea and tick treatments prevent our furry friends from dying from tick paralysis. These understandings have been developed through controlled studies over a number of years, investigating the impact of different factors (Australian Bureau of Statistics, n.d.; SAS Institute Inc, n.d.b). As research increases and more studies find data that confirms or denies the causation, the relationship gets stronger and the cause becomes more attributable.

Many times when correlation is seen, causation is assumed. I recently saw a funny meme on LinkedIn where there was a collapsing tin roof with a buckled metal post, and there was a cat sitting on the roof; the image implied causation, but it is actually just correlation (or coincidence) that the cat was sitting in a spot that made it look like it had caused the buckling of the metal post.

It is important to know the difference between the two and be prepared to check your own assumptions about causation, and those of your colleagues. If they jump to an assumption about causation, ask how they know one causes the other. What other information do they have? Or explore different reasons why the data might be saying what you think it is saying. Don't be satisfied with an explanation that is quick and causal – our organisations and organisational challenges are rarely that simple, and to be honest, if it sounds too good to be true, it probably is!

What data matters?

Sorting through the noise of all the millions (literally) of data points and determining what you should pay attention to is a significant challenge – especially if you feel you're not a numbers person. Later in this chapter, there are some steps you might choose to follow to help you ascertain what is most important to you. First, though, let's unpack some of the common data types and figures that we see regularly, to ensure that we all have a consistent understanding of what these numbers are.

A 2018 *Forbes* article by Adrian Bridgwater categorised organisational data into 13 main categories:

1. Big data
2. Structured, unstructured, semi-structured data
3. Time-stamped data
4. Machine data
5. Spatiotemporal data
6. Open data
7. Dark data
8. Real time data
9. Genomics data

10. Operational data
11. High-dimensional data
12. Unverified outdated data
13. Translytic data.

If that list creates rising anxiety for you, don't worry – we are not going to talk about all of them. Your organisation will have access to different amounts and types of data, but of most interest to us is the operational and translytic data. Operational data is the data that provides information from within the organisation itself, largely to do with the operations. Translytic data is a combination of transactions and analytics, meaning that it is the data that is generated in real time that can be leveraged to provide insights into the organisation.

Let's now unpack a few of the key metrics that are often used by different organisations. They may not all relate to your work specifically, but they are all used extensively across different organisations. Before we get started, there are a few key terms that are useful to know at this point. They are:

- **Revenue:** The amount of money your business turns over in a year, without taking into consideration any expenses (think 'the amount that gets paid into the business account').
- **Expenses:** All the money that needs to leave your business to pay 'bills'. This may include things like wages, taxes, leases, operating costs and manufacturing costs.
- **Profit:** The dollar value once all expenses have been subtracted from the revenue.

The glossary at the end of this book has a summary of more key terminology that you might find useful.

Profit margin

Profit margin is a key metric that is used in many businesses. It's a measure of the percentage of the revenue that is kept as profit, after all expenses have been accounted for. Profit margin can be much more useful than talking about revenue or profit in dollars – it might be nice to know that your business has an annual turnover of $20 million, but if your expenses are out of hand, you may not be making any profit from that at all. All $20 million might be heading straight back out of the organisation to pay bills, or you might actually be spending more than you are earning.

The other reason that the profit margin (a percentage rather than a dollar value) is useful is because it allows you to compare the percentage across different time periods. If you only work with profit in dollars, it becomes very difficult to compare when you have variations in earnings or expenses. If, for example, you had a turnover of $250,000 in one quarter and you outlaid $200,000 in expenses, your profit would be $50,000. The following quarter, if you had $320,000 in turnover and $270,000 in expenses, your profit would be the same in terms of a dollar value, but not the same as a proportion of your overall revenue.

In the first quarter, your profit margin would be 20 per cent, but the second quarter it would be 15.6 per cent. So, while your turnover was more in the second quarter, and your profit had the same dollar value, your expenses rose and therefore you had a smaller profit margin.

To calculate the profit margin, you first need to establish all the money coming into the organisation – that is your revenue. You then need to calculate all the money leaving to pay bills – those are your expenses.

$$\text{Profit in dollars} = \text{Revenue} - \text{expenses}$$

$$\text{Profit margin} = \frac{\text{Profit in dollars}}{\text{Revenue}} \times 100$$

Different industries have different expectations around profit margin. While the target figures differ depending on where you look, if you are in the unfortunate position of having expenses that are greater than your income that means you're running at a loss, and your profit margin will be a negative number. If this is the case, it is important to think about how you can increase the money coming in and decrease the money going out. Kappel (2020) proposes potential ways to do this, including reducing waste, dropping options or products that do not sell well, raising prices and upselling or cross-selling. Essentially, when the money in versus the money out is equal, there will be no profit; and when you are able to bring in more than you are spending, that is when you start to make a profit.

Customer preferences data

Another key type of information that you'll have access to in your organisation is about your customers themselves. Depending on your industry, this data will have a different impact or be used in different ways. However, whatever role you are in and wherever you currently find yourself working, data on the people who buy from you or engage your services provides key information and feedback. As the PwC Annual Global CEO survey found, 'customer data that feeds new value propositions, new and improved experiences and new revenue models is how winners will distance themselves from the pack' (in Busby, 2019).

The interest in customer data has recently increased. Monty Hamilton from PwC (2017) said that a key turning point in the collection and use of customer data was Edwina Dunn and Clive Humby's development of Tesco's Clubcard rewards program in the United Kingdom. When small business owners Dunn and Humby presented the idea and software to the Tesco directors, the chairman, Lord MacLaurin, famously said, 'What scares me about this is that you know more about my customers after three months than I know after 30 years' (Smale, 2014). Dunn and Humby managed to convince the board that they could work out customers' spending habits and preferences, and within a year, Tesco doubled its market share. Smale reports that the Tesco Clubcard was the first supermarket loyalty card in the world.

PwC's 22nd Annual Global CEO survey in 2019 found that 94 per cent of respondents believed customer and client preferences and needs were critical or important (Busby, 2019). The information that you collect on customers will depend on your aims and what you intend to do with the information once you have it. In the last month I have experienced the following examples of perception data collection:

- After having a telephone conversation with a utilities company, they sent me an email asking 'On a scale of 0 to 10 (10 being the highest), how likely are you to recommend [Company A] to friends and family?'
- After an online engagement with a technology support company, I received a survey link via email, titled 'We'd love to hear your thoughts.' The preface of the survey form said, 'We love feedback. We work hard to continuously improve our service, so we'd love to hear what's working and where we can do better. Your answers are completely confidential, and your feedback will help us make [Company B] even better for you and others!'
- After a recent online purchase, Company C sent a follow-up email to ask me to rate the product purchased on their website, and to review it on Google, both to help future buyers and to promote their product and brand.

These three examples provide tangible examples of ways that different organisations are already collecting data from their customers about what they think about a product or service. The idea is that this feedback provides information to the organisation or team about their work.

However, too often I work with organisations that have no clear strategy for using the information they glean from these surveys, meaning it potentially goes to waste. There is so much possibility in the information collected from customers about their perceptions – you can use it as feedback about your teams, or to start a conversation about adjusting processes or structures. It can indicate the products that are working more than others, and why. If used well, it can maximise profits and minimise your focus on products and services that are not selling or being utilised well. But you need to have a systematic process for collecting, reporting on and acting on the data.

Customer demographic data

Another area of consumer data that many organisations have access to is demographics – information about subsets of the broader customer base, including geographic location, age, gender and so on. Some organisations choose to collect information in this way, as for some fields it is really useful – for example, to establish the age range of people who shop or use the service, average spending per customer, highest engagement and buyer location. This information could be collected in person (directly), or online (either directly or indirectly).

A local clothes store that collects postcodes from each customer is an example of in-person direct collection. At the point of sale, the cashier asks for the postcode and enters it in the system. The franchise owner collects the data to send to head office, and it is used to establish buyer trends. If the company were to expand or open new stores in the future, it would have an idea of where it might open a new store.

When you sign up to a mailing list of your favourite store, this is an example of an online direct collection. By entering your information at registration, you are providing data to the company that helps it learn who its target market should be and where its customers live. It can use this to inform decisions about lines, products and marketing strategies. They could also use this information to target advertising – for example, an insurance comparison company in Australia recently promoted on billboards that more than 2000 'Jessicas' had used its service.

Using Google Analytics to ascertain patterns in online website activity is an example of online indirect collection. You can view thousands (if not millions) of data points through a range of visualisations on Google Analytics for your website, including geographic location, average session duration (how long people stay on your website), bounce rate (the percentage of people who land on the website and do nothing) and the number of sessions per sub-page on your website. If you can work out what is important and how to get the information, it could potentially be very useful in helping guide actions and focus.

Again, all of these data points are potentially useful – they could direct your attention to areas requiring consideration, and inspire action. However, if you don't have a plan in place, don't have a strategy for what data you are going to pay attention to and why, and don't understand what the data means or how it could be used, it is a wasted opportunity.

Technology can make data much easier to use. There has been a surge in the number of companies working in this space to attempt to automate some of this work. PwC's 24th Annual Global CEO survey found that 'companies on the leading edge are more deeply embedding AI [artificial intelligence] in customer-focused applications, back-office applications and risk management—while addressing algorithmic bias so that stakeholders trust the outputs' (PwC, 2021). However, this technology requires time, effort and resources to establish.

Triangulating data

Regardless of the types of data that are important to you, you must understand and implement the idea of triangulation wherever possible. Triangulation means consulting three or more data sources to identify trends and guide your decision-making, rather than just relying on a single data source (Jick, 1979; Thurmond, 2001).

Triangulation was historically used in navigation, prior to GPS and marine radio, to help a ship's captain ascertain their position on a map when they only had access to a map and a compass. If the captain saw a landmark on the land and identified it on their map (for example, the steeple in figure 2.2), they could use their compass to take a bearing of their position relative to the landmark, and draw a reverse bearing (line) onto their map. This was somewhat useful, because the line gave an indication of the boat's position on the map; however, it did not give a lot of context or a specific position. This is because, even with an accurate bearing, the boat could be 50 metres from the landmark or 500 metres from the landmark. The bearing would be the same because it is simply a measure of the angle relative to true north.

If the captain took a second bearing (to, say, the lighthouse in figure 2.2) they could draw a second bearing (line) on the map to establish a more accurate indication of the boat's position. This is more useful than a single bearing, because the captain now has two lines on the map (one from the steeple and one from the lighthouse) and hopefully these two lines cross to indicate where the boat might be. Unfortunately, however, a lot could still go wrong – there could have been an error with misreading the compass on either occasion; either of the backbearing lines might have been drawn incorrectly onto the map; or the crew might have forgotten to anchor in between the two readings, meaning the boat drifted (and who knows how far?).

When it is possible to collect a third piece of data (like the cliff in figure 2.2), the position is triangulated – the three lines on the map create a triangle. For a ship's captain, the accuracy of the pieces of data will be conveyed in the size of the triangle – if they did a pretty good job of taking the bearings, drawing on the map and remembering to anchor, the triangle will be quite small. The more inaccurate one of the lines, the larger the triangle will be on the map.

Figure 2.2: Example of three triangulated lines on a map

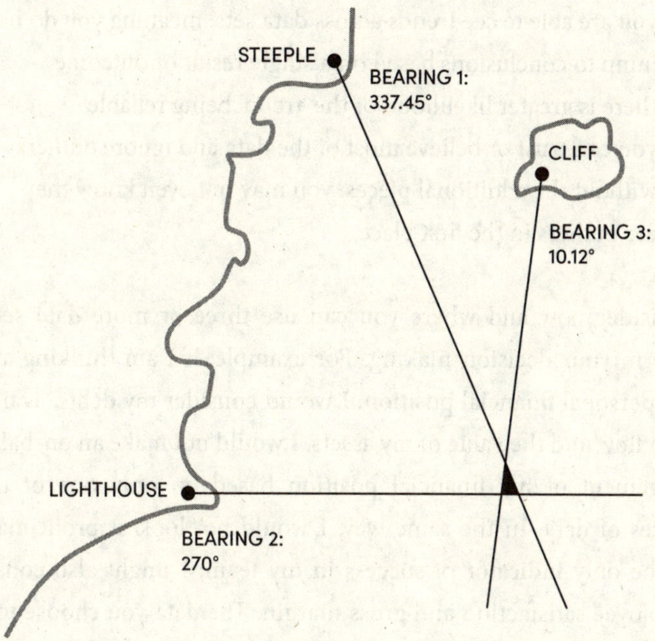

These days, triangulation is still used extensively in research. Just like in the map example, triangulating in research ensures that data is collected from multiple sources, or (for example) multiple stakeholder groups, so that the trends and lessons that emerge across the sets of data are more reliable and applicable. Triangulation improves 'the accuracy of ... judgements by collecting different kinds of data bearing on the same phenomenon' (Thurmond, 2001). If different people in different organisations are telling you similar things, you can confidently report on these trends, and they are potentially relevant to other (or similar) organisations. In a business context, triangulation is just as important for us as it was for the captain of a pre-GPS ship.

Having three pieces of organisational data means:

- you are able to see trends across data sets, meaning you do not jump to conclusions based on a single result or outcome
- there is greater likelihood of the 'trend' being reliable
- you can trust or believe most of the data and ignore outliers – without the additional pieces, you may not even know they are outliers in the first place.

Consider how and where you can use three or more data sets to inform your decision-making. For example, if I am thinking about my personal financial position, I would consider my debts, available cash flow and the value of my assets. I would not make an on-balance judgement of my financial position based on only one of those pieces of data. In the same way, I would not look at profit margin as the only indicator of success in my team; I might also consider employee satisfaction and gross margin. The data you choose to use to triangulate will differ depending on your context and the inquiry or analysis that you are doing, but it is important to choose data that will give you the best indication of what you are looking into. More information about choosing the right data can be found later in this chapter.

Point-in-time versus longitudinal data

Another factor to consider is point-in-time data versus longitudinal data – the differences between them, and the usefulness of looking at both.

Point-in-time data is just that – it is a metric, measurement or data point that represents a single time period. If, for example, you were looking at revenue for your current month or the profit margin for the quarter, that is a single, point-in-time measure.

Many data sets that you have access to can be considered longitudinally, or over time. Rather than just looking at your revenue for the current month, longitudinal measures require two or more data points and track how that metric is performing over different time periods. Consider for example your revenue per month. When you compare at least two monthly revenue figures to each other, that is when you are starting to look at your data longitudinally. If you can do that for a period of 3, 6 or 12 months, that's even more useful.

There are many benefits to looking at data longitudinally rather than as a single metric:

- You have a context for the number you are looking at – otherwise you may not know whether the current result is high, low or record breaking.
- You can compare results and consider trends over time.
- You can look at trends for different times of the year and compare them to a similar period – rather than a single result, which might fluctuate considerably.

Being able to look at the distance your business has travelled, track growth or decline over time and compare similar time periods or parts of the year gives you more contextually relevant and appropriate measures to inform your decision-making, rather than looking at a single metric alone. If your sales or operations are seasonal (like a swimwear company or an alpine ski resort), it is more important that you compare the current period with the same period 12 and 24 months ago, rather than comparing your current revenue to your revenue for the previous quarter.

Trends become obvious when you look at data over time. Identifying a trend means simply noticing that a metric is improving, staying consistent or declining. Depending on the metric you are viewing, you will want different things to be happening in the longitudinal data – for example, you might like to see revenue increase, expenses decrease and productivity stay consistent if your factory is working at capacity. However, it is important to point out that a trend is not two points on a graph (Graban, 2019). Think back to your previous learning about triangulation – if your sales figures are up this month compared to last month, this is not a trend; but if your sales have increased steadily over the last three months, that *is* a trend. The reality is that your revenue, expenses, profit and sales will fluctuate – they will not consistently increase, decrease or stay the same. That's why one point that is higher or lower than the last is not a trend – wait for a third piece of data before you even think to start making statements about trends.

If you are looking at longitudinal data that jumps around considerably, one strategy to make sense of this data is using a moving average (Glen, 2021). This technique was used heavily throughout the COVID-19 pandemic, when daily numbers of cases, hospitalisations and deaths moved up and down, sometimes quite considerably, from one day to the next. Instead of showing the raw data, many news organisations and reporting bodies used moving averages – usually across the previous 7 or 14 days. The moving average graph shows the average of the metric over the number of days (7 or 14 in this instance), rather than the raw data from each day. During the pandemic, this reduced the chance that someone would claim an improving or worsening situation based on only one day's data. It also smoothed the graph, making the trend more easily readable. The moving average is also used extensively in stocks and cryptocurrency, due to the high variability and regular changes in values.

Statistical significance is another factor to consider. Whenever you analyse data, you want to be able to ascertain which data and changes are significant and which are not (Gallo, 2016). As you will see in the next chapter, it can be easy to manipulate graphs of longitudinal data to make it look as though there are greater or lesser changes, depending on what you do with the vertical axis. However, if you understand the notion of statistical significance, you will view and engage with the data in a more well-rounded and holistic way, meaning that if there is manipulation in the graph, you will notice.

As Sapirstein (n.d.) said, 'A tremendously told story that is rooted in unfounded, statistically insignificant data is, unfortunately, not a good story. Touting information that stems from statistically insignificant data can drive actions that end up being a waste of time, energy and money.' Generally, something is statistically significant if it changes more than 5 per cent from the previous figure (that is, a 5 per cent difference – *not* a difference of five percentage points). This percentage change is not a hard-and-fast rule, though. It is about working out what works for your business, what you accept as being significant, and making decisions accordingly.

Longitudinal data analysis also allows for interpolation and extrapolation if either are necessary or useful (see figure 2.3). Interpolation is the ability to look within the end data points and predict one value from another. This is useful if you want to use the data that you already have to predict a value. For example, you could use interpolation to consider the cost of buying a certain amount of product – or the other way around, to work out the amount of product you can afford to buy, based on the money you have to spend.

Interpolation is when you use the data you have and look inside it to see the relationships.

Extrapolation, on the other hand, allows for prediction outside of the window of data that you have access to. If you have a longitudinal view, extrapolation allows you to predict a value based on another *before* the first data point, or *after* the last data point. Forecasters use a form of extrapolation to predict the price of cryptocurrency five and 10 years from now. If your business is expanding, you could use extrapolation to ascertain potential increased employee numbers or output.

Longitudinal data has a lot of uses in business. By understanding what it can do for you, you can choose what works for you and capitalise on the benefits.

Figure 2.3: Interpolation and extrapolation

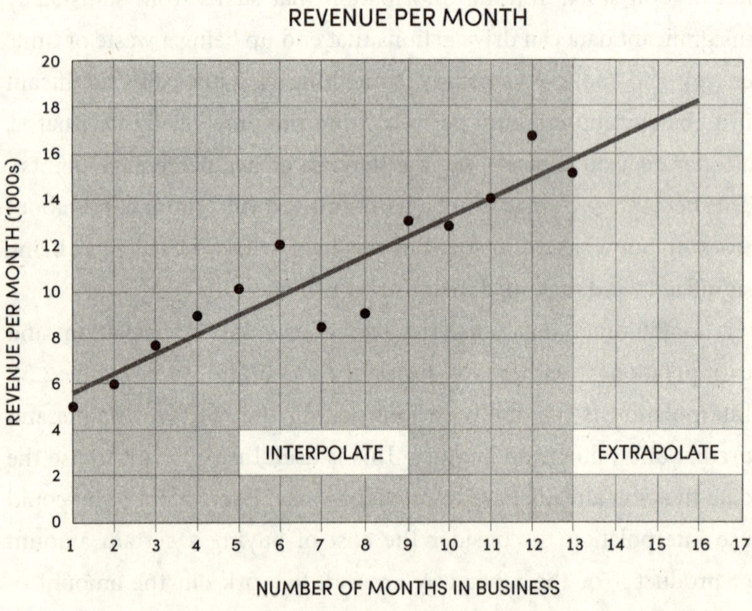

Qualitative data

Qualitative data is the second major type of data that you'll have access to. Broadly, it is the data that is *not* numbers. It might include things like the list of products on offer, the different roles in your organisation or feedback from customers. It differs from quantitative data in that is not based on numbers, and you can't easily and definitively summarise the information and build graphs and charts based on it.

There are two broad types of qualitative information: categorical and ordinal. Ordinal data (the clue is in the name) is information that has some sort of order. If you offer different sizes of product (for example, small, medium and large), or ask employees in an exit interview to what extent they agree or disagree with a series of statements (for example, strongly agree, agree, neutral, disagree or strongly disagree), these categories are ordinal. There is an order to the responses and one can be ranked higher or lower than another. On the other hand, categorical data fits into categories where there is no set order – for example, the different types of products you offer, the types of delivery partners you use or the countries your customers come from. In categorical data, there is no 'hierarchy' or order to the groups of information.

Text responses or descriptions are a type of qualitative data you probably have access to. These provide additional detail and description – for example, about processes and procedures, or a person's experience with the company. While you may not be able to categorise this information as categorical or ordinal, text responses such as those that come from employee or client perception surveys (where people are asked to explain why they would recommend your company to others, or why they enjoy working with you) are beneficial because they provide great feedback and explanations of some of the quantitative data.

If, for example, customers rate your company on a five-point scale on Google reviews, this quantitative information allows you to look at trends in different areas, or over time, and easily compare how your organisation is tracking in different locations. You can look at the number of five-star or one-star reviews that you have, and see your average score out of five from all reviewers. However, the text response also gives valuable detail and feedback on the client's experience. If a client is exceptionally happy with the service received, the qualitative response can be useful in identifying the things that are working well. It could also possibly provide you with testimonial explaining why others should choose to use or buy your product or service. Conversely, if a text explanation outlines challenges that a customer faced, problems they had or reasons they weren't happy with your product or service, this provides useful information about what has gone wrong. Sure, one person's Google review *is* only one person's Google review, but it is an instant opportunity to respond publicly and build your brand, *and* if it is a consistent pattern or recurring theme, it provides an opportunity to reflect on the feedback and adjust your approach if needed.

Organisations are increasingly seeking to gather feedback from clients, customers, employees or volunteers via survey, where they ask a combination of qualitative and quantitative questions. If you were to consider how much qualitative versus quantitative data you should collect in these surveys, I recommend you first consider how and why you are asking the questions that you are. The Google review example is limited, in that customers only have the option to provide one quantitative response and one qualitative response. However, I have worked with organisations who had staff perception surveys containing five or more (even 15 to 20!) qualitative, text-based response opportunities. While it is beneficial to understand the 'why' from the people you are surveying, every question you add is another qualitative data set, and this means additional time and effort is required for analysis. If, for example, you ask one qualitative question of your 100 employees, you have 100 responses to read, analyse and use. If you ask a second question, you double the responses and you now have 200 responses to read, interpret and analyse. If you ask a third question, you now have 300 responses. I could keep going… (but I don't suggest you do!) It is significantly more difficult to have qualitative, text-based questions in a survey compared with quantitative, so use them wisely. I tend to recommend that you only put one in a survey, but two or three are possible if you have a really good reason to ask the questions, and you have a strategy for how you are going to analyse and use the information.

Qualitative data is beneficial in that it allows you to view your business, risk, processes and impact through response categories that can be organised and compared, or through text responses or comments that provide detail and explanation of the quantitative data. It provides the additional context that quantitative data misses, and explains the 'why' of a quantitative response. The downside: qualitative data is harder to visualise, as it does not always easily and readily fit into graphs and diagrams to support data storytelling. Also, text responses take considerably longer to analyse and use than numbers. If, for example, you get hundreds of Google reviews each week, the time taken to read, analyse, respond, and think about the data storytelling from the text responses is much more significant than tracking your overall rating or score out of five.

Thematic analysis

Thematic analysis is one way of dealing with and making sense of qualitative data – but beware, it can be very time consuming. It can be a useful process to go through, but it is important that you weigh up the time commitment first, before collecting the qualitative data or engaging in the process.

As the name suggests, thematic analysis is where you look for and analyse themes or broader ideas in qualitative data. It is useful because it allows you to look for overarching or emerging challenges, bright spots or areas to focus on in the data, without losing the detail of the brilliant descriptions, explanations and specific information provided in the survey or interview responses.

Thematic analysis is not something most people have experience with, and to be honest, had I not completed a doctorate that relied on qualitative data, I probably wouldn't have been exposed to it either. In terms of a model of thematic analysis, I use Braun and Clarke's (2006) framework and six stages, as I find it a comprehensive and logical way of approaching the challenge. Braun and Clarke (2006) define thematic analysis as 'a method for identifying, analysing, and reporting patterns (themes) within data. It minimally organises and describes your data set it in (rich) detail. However, it also often goes further than this, and interprets various aspects of the research topic.' In short, thematic analysis allows you to think about the various themes in the data, label and categorise the data, and find the most frequent and consistent themes.

Thematic analysis can be performed as a manual process (where you use the tools you already have access to, such as Microsoft Word and Excel) or through an analysis program (such as NVivo or SPSS). Both analysis programs are good (once you know how to use them) and are specifically designed for this purpose; however, they are not necessary if you are not a researcher or if you are not planning on engaging in a lot of qualitative analysis. You can, in much the same way, manually code themes in Microsoft Word, and the outcomes or output of your analysis can be exactly the same.

I tend to simplify Braun and Clarke's process into four main phases:

1. Identify themes in the data
2. Code themes in the data
3. Consider the prevalence of the themes across all the data
4. Report the findings.

The additional steps in their process relate to reviewing, adjusting and modifying themes or codes through the process. While I agree that it is important that you continue to review and evolve the themes throughout your analysis (and go back and recode if/when that is necessary), I believe this needs to happen as a continuous process throughout, rather than a definitive stage. There is also an expectation here that before you begin, all of your data is in text format, preferably in similar documents or the same document. If you have interviews, you may need to have these typed up first, and/or export the data from its storage place.

Once you have access to all the data that you are going to work with in text format, you can start with step 1. Think about the broader notion of what you want to achieve – what are you trying to find out from the data? What are you interested in learning more about? For example, are you trying to identify consistent errors in your manufacturing process? Are you trying to identify human resource challenges within your organisation? Or are you seeking feedback from your customers on their experience?

Whatever your focus is, the next task is to plan out the codes that you will use through the analysis process that sit underneath these big-ticket items, as these themes will help you answer your initial inquiry. To do this, first think about the question you are trying to answer, and plan general responses, codes or 'buckets' of responses that the text responses could fit into. Don't get caught up in the detail of the individual responses at this stage, but ensure you are happy with the codes. Be okay with the fact that the codes are deliberately broader and more vague than the text responses – you could never create specific codes for every response, and it wouldn't help you analyse trends if you did. Table 2.1 lists some example qualitative questions along with possible codes that could be used for them.

Table 2.1: Sample codes that sit within an overall qualitative question

Qualitative questions	*Response codes*
What are some of the consistent errors with the product?	1. Manufacturing defect 2. Usability 3. Reliability 4. Life of product
What is it like working at our organisation?	1. Generally very rewarding 2. Satisfactory employee experience 3. Disappointed with employee experience 4. Comments about additional support/ development opportunities
Overall, how would you rate your experience of dealing with our organisation?	1. Generally very positive 2. Quite positive 3. Neutral 4. Somewhat negative 5. Very negative 6. Issue with customer service 7. Issue with product 8. Issue with process 9. Issue with price

As you can see in the table, the codes apply to broad responses survey respondents make. You will lose some of the detail of specific responses along the way, and be forced to make a decision about which category the response fits into; but the ultimate goal of this analysis is to see broad themes across all responses, and use specific quotes or experiences to provide additional detail when you need to.

Keep in mind that you can give a single response more than one code. For example, if a customer had a particularly poor experience, you might code them as 'very negative', and if it specifically related to customer service, you could also code it as 'issue with customer service'.

Step 2 of the thematic analysis process requires you to use these codes and apply them to the data. Read through the responses and use your chosen software to code the responses. To 'code' them, highlight the phrase or sentence that applies to your code, and either add a tag (in NVivo) or a comment balloon (in Microsoft Word) so there is a record of the data sitting within that theme.

In Microsoft Word, you can choose to code the individual phrase that applies to the code (see figure 2.4) or highlight the entire comment and add in all the codes that apply (see figure 2.5).

As you go through this process, you should add additional codes to your code list as new things emerge (for example, if you start to see a lot of people talking about team dynamics, you might add this as a code), but you will need to go back and make sure you have not missed any previous responses that could have been coded as 'team dynamics'.

Figure 2.4: An example of coded qualitative data in Microsoft Word, with the relevant unique phrase highlighted and single code in a comment balloon on the right-hand side

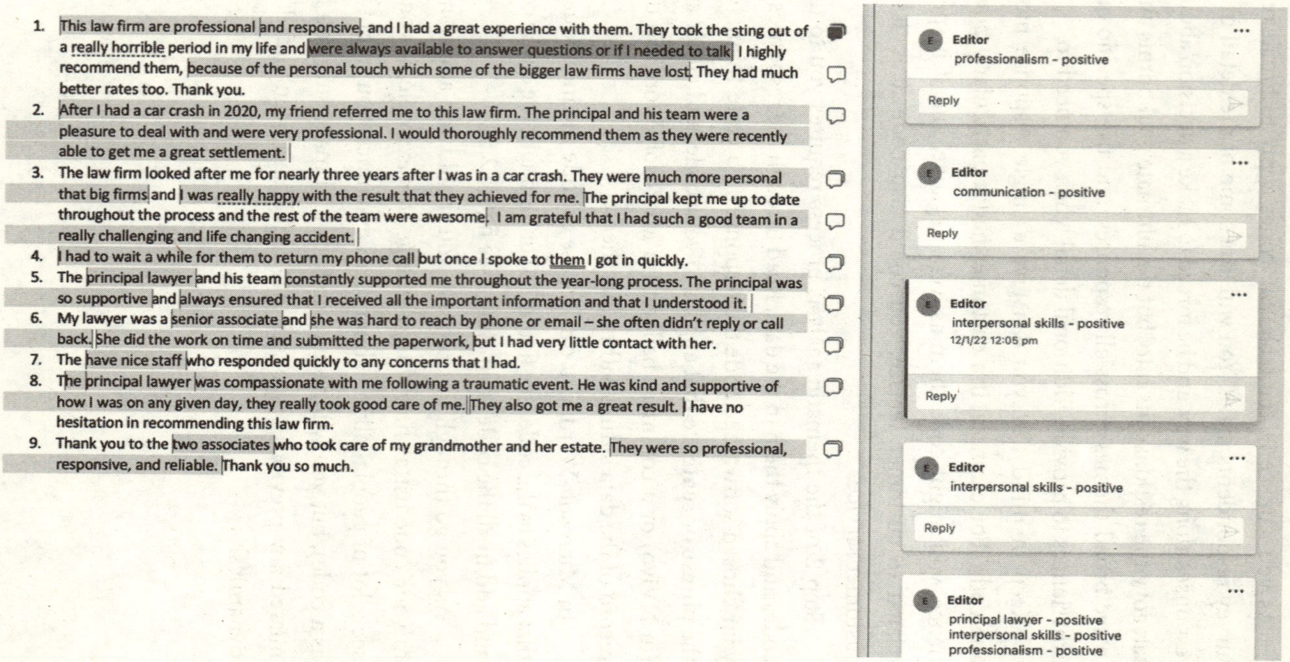

Figure 2.5: An example of coded qualitative data in Microsoft Word, with the whole comment highlighted and all relevant codes entered in a single comment balloon on the right-hand side

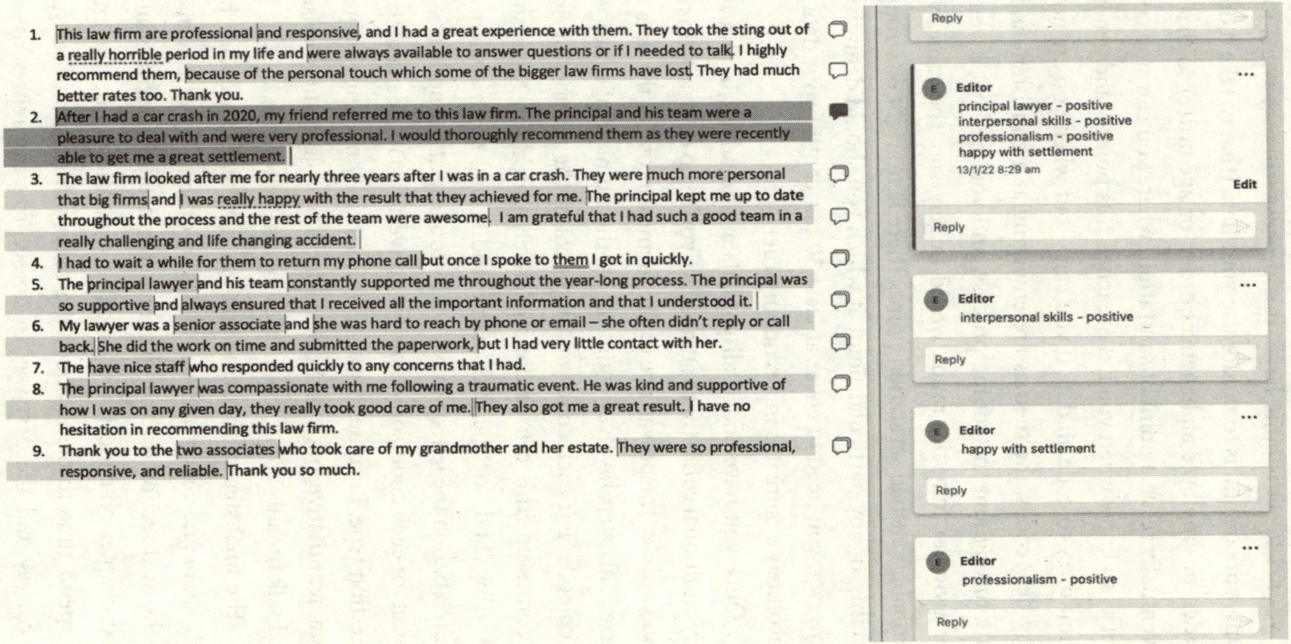

If your data set is quite large, this process will take you a long time. One workaround is to randomise your data (that is, take it out of date order, or employee alphabetical order, or age order) so that you will eventually reach a point of saturation, where you can stop coding. It's tricky to know when you have reached this point – and generally you should try to code all data if you can – but when you are not adding any new codes, the themes are emerging at a consistent and similar rate throughout the coding process, and you feel that if you worked for twice as long the ratios would largely stay the same, you have probably reached saturation point. There is no right or wrong way to do this, or any particular point at which you should definitively stop; however, you need to cover at least 30 per cent of your data set, and absolutely ensure it is in a random order.

Once you have coded all your data, and added in and reviewed any additional codes that you need to, you're up to step 3. this is where you consider the prevalence of the themes across all the data that you have. This step involves counting up the number of times you used each code. For each code you might count the number of times that it comes up (this can be done relatively quickly in Microsoft Word by using 'find' for the code name and seeing the prevalence in the search bar on the left, or in NVivo by looking at the node tree and the count for each code), or you might convert this to a percentage for the question type. In some ways, this is essentially making the qualitative data quantitative, but it is the best way to be able to summarise results and talk broadly about the themes that are emerging.

The final step of thematic analysis is where you decide how you will share and report these findings to others. There is a discussion in the next section on how to choose the data to prioritise, and in the next chapter on choosing the right visualisations, but it is important to spend time thinking about the main information that you want to convey and the best way to do so. You can represent much of your qualitative data and thematic analysis in numerical scores and percentages, but you may also want to include specific, noteworthy quotes that provide a unique insight, or focus on the use of keywords. Infographics are one good way of combining key messages that emerge from the data, and provide opportunity for both qualitative and quantitative data.

I recently put together an infographic for a training organisation as an example of a way that they could share survey feedback with their community. In the infographic, I used quantitative data in average scores out of 10, the overall percentages for satisfaction questions (100 per cent being the maximum), text responses about the key learnings for individuals, and keywords that appeared most frequently in participants' responses. There was a deliberate mix of graphs, fuel gauge images and lollipop charts – all had a different purpose and told a different story. While there are thousands of ways to convey similar information, it is important that you think about what is the cleanest and most useful way of representing the data and sharing it with your intended audience.

Another way of representing qualitative data is in a word cloud. You might think word clouds are a little elementary; however, they can be a useful way of representing large amounts of qualitative information. To create a word cloud, you upload or import the text responses (there are plenty of free tools for this available online) and the tool displays the words in a list, according to frequency, as represented by the size of the text in the generated word cloud. The largest words are those that appear most often, and the smallest words appear less frequently. There are usually a few levels of text sizes to indicate different frequencies.

If you want to use a word cloud, or look for the prevalence of keywords, there are a couple of points to be mindful of. First, there are plenty of useless words in qualitative data that do not enhance the understanding of the content itself. For example, when I entered this book manuscript into a word cloud program (see figure 2.6), it displayed words such as 'can', 'use', 'will', 'need' and so on. These words only serve to complicate the word cloud rather than enhancing understanding of the key trends in the book. Word cloud programs allow you to delete words that do not help the purpose of the word cloud, and I strongly encourage you to spend the time to remove these words to clean up your summary and visualisation. There were over 2500 words in the word cloud list for the book; all of the words that only appear a handful of times are not useful – they serve only as distractors and lessen the impact.

Figure 2.6: Word cloud of this book's text from wordclouds.com

The other thing worth checking before you publish your word cloud for others to see is the consistency of spelling of words in your list, as well as plurals. For example, in my word cloud of this manuscript, 'visualisation' and 'visualisations' appeared as separate entries; and where I wrote 'well-being' instead of 'wellbeing', the program didn't recognise that they are the same word. The problem this creates is that if you have different words with different frequencies, you can't truly see the impact of keywords if there are multiple entries, and consequently the scores and text size will be inaccurate.

Qualitative data has a lot to offer an organisation or business looking to harness the power of data; however, you need to be deliberate and discerning in your collection of qualitative data to ensure that the return on investment is worthwhile.

Knowing which data to choose or prioritise

One of the key challenges you're likely to face is that it's not always clear which types of data you should be paying attention to. If your organisation is like most, you are most likely inundated with vast amounts of data and it is unrealistic to assume that you (or others) can use it all. It's important to know that you need to prioritise your focus and inquiry, and ensure that you are using the data that is most relevant and important.

Within the same organisation, different people in different roles will prioritise and use different data in different ways; and that is absolutely necessary. If the bottom line of your role is profit, then of course you need to predominantly focus on profit value and profit margin; however, these are not the only two metrics that you should rely on, and they are not the only data other employees in your organisation will use. As discussed in the section on triangulation, regardless of your role, you need to draw on several data sources to form a holistic picture of what is happening for your team and organisation.

You should focus on data that you and your team have control over or some responsibility for. There will be a lot of data available to you – and a lot of it might be interesting – but you and your team may have no control or influence over what the majority of the data does. For example, hotels often use a 'heads on beds' or occupancy percentage to indicate the number of bookings they have and the current numbers of guests in the resort. While this might be interesting and useful to keep an eye on, the leader of the hotel's cleaning team, for example, would not focus on this type of data, because their work does not directly affect it. There are other, more appropriate types of information that would be better suited for the cleaning team to monitor, such as room cleanliness reviews, cleaning turnaround times, logistics and process data, and staff satisfaction, as all of these would better guide and inform the cleaning team about their work and progress.

If you are unsure of the types of data that you should be paying attention to, consider working through the following steps:

1. Brainstorm a list of all the data you have available. Consider qualitative and quantitative data; think about big-picture statistics and more fine-tuned information. Make a physical list somewhere that you can refer to later (either on paper or electronically).
2. Think about your role and responsibilities and consider all the types of data that are necessary for you to do your job well, and know you are having an impact. Focus on the data that relates directly to you and your team – that is, data you have some impact on. Highlight or select these data types in your list. Make sure you do not include any metrics that you have no control over.

3. Rank the data types you chose in step 2 in order of importance, from highest to lowest. You could think about this through the lens of 'what can't you ignore?' and put these things at the top of the list.
4. Once you have your hierarchy list, annotate each data type to explain the use/necessity of the information. How do you use it, why is it important and how can you influence it? Change the priority order of your data types if necessary to ensure your list is in the right order.
5. More brains are better than one. Share the list with a colleague, or your team, and talk them through the process you have been through. Listen to their recommendations and make any necessary adjustments. Add in data types that you believe are useful, and shuffle your order of priority if you need to. Keep in mind, though, this is your (or your team's) list – do not be swayed by different information that is important to others. This is about creating your own list.
6. Use this list to focus your work on data literacy. Do you or your team know what each of the metrics means and have at least a basic understanding of how it is calculated? Do you understand the context of what a good, average or low result means, and do you know what you should be aiming for? Think about training that might help build data literacy in this space, because the next steps through to data storytelling cannot happen unless you understand the numbers you are dealing with.

Developing data literacy around each of the different types of data may be difficult, and it will take time. In some cases, a quick explanation from a colleague or a short YouTube tutorial might help build understanding. But it may not be a speedy process if maths is not your forte; if there are a few levels of complex calculations involved;

or if there are different values of categories and threshold cut-offs. It is time consuming, but it so vital.

Once you develop your (or your team's) data literacy with these data types, it is worth going back and reviewing your list every year. As technology evolves and organisations change, other metrics will become more important, or they may move in their position on your list. That is fine, and to be expected, but remember to stay up-to-date with learning about the new key data types. Don't be worried about having to learn about new metrics in the future – it is an ongoing and evolving process and always will be.

Data plan

An increasingly common way to prioritise the data that your team or organisation focuses on is to develop a data plan. A data plan is useful because it allows you to critically reflect on and review the different types of data available in your organisation – but it also allows you to think about what you actually need to pay attention to. Leaders that I have gone through this process with have enjoyed the thinking itself, as it helps build clarity around what you collect and why, and helps focus your attention on key information. Once you have a draft data plan, it is also useful to engage other team leaders and members in the conversation; this provides all employees clarity about the metrics they need to value and utilise in their roles.

A data plan is necessary because over time, the data you have available in your organisation will increase exponentially. New data types and sources will be added and layered on top of one another progressively over time, with very few data sets being removed. (Sometimes some metrics are broken down and further unpacked, but data tends not to disappear or be removed.) Because there is too much data for you to ever use or action it all, it is worth going through the process of zooming out and thinking about what helps you achieve you strategic priorities, what you need to use and prioritise, and how you expect each of the metrics to be used.

There is no single right way to write a data plan, but there are a few things to think about when you are constructing it. These include:

- How will you group data in your plan? Will you group by employee, team, focus area or data type?
- How will you represent the idea of triangulation in your plan? How can you show that multiple data sets should inform decision-making?
- Do you need to include information about the way trends and insights or actions are communicated, and if so, to whom?
- Do you need to include additional information about data entry, storage or security?
- What is most important to you in the plan? If the teams and purpose are most important, put those columns to the left. If targets are most important, put them as far left as you can. However, if your targets are less important than all the other elements, move that column over to the right.

Table 2.2 overleaf provides a sample data plan template.

Table 2.2: Sample data plan template

Team	*Data sets*	*Collected/ analysed by*	*Why it is useful*	*Targets*	*Analysis required*	*Associated actions*	*Communication required*	*Data storage/ security*
Sales	Sales value Geographical sales information Sales online versus store	Sales lead	Provides information about where sales are coming from	Increase sales by 15% in the next quarter	Compare month to month sales figures Compare to Q1 and to Q2 last year	Take to next sales meeting Present potential options for growth	Overall trends and distance from goals (sales team) Summary trends (C-suite)	Hosted on sales platform. All sales staff have access to team metrics.
HR	Staff absenteeism Staff turnover Staff satisfaction survey	HR data analyst	Provides information on staff morale and culture	Maintain absenteeism rate below 5% Maintain staff satisfaction above 4.7	Triangulate results to determine current level of staff satisfaction Compare results for month and identify trends	Take findings to wellbeing committee Report results to Director of HR Plan next steps	Share actions and decisions from wellbeing committee with employees	Survey responses deidentified on staff shared drive. Exit meeting notes kept on employee file only.

In this chapter we've dug into data literacy – specifically the types of qualitative and quantitative data available and the ways that this data can be used. The first and fundamental step of using data well is having a solid data literacy – once you understand the numbers and what they mean, you can begin to use this understanding to take the next steps. This includes understanding correlation versus causation, triangulation, point-in-time and longitudinal data, and knowing how to select the right data to focus on.

If your aim is to get to the point of data storytelling, you next need to take your data literacy and apply it to be able to read, interpret and create data visualisations that make the data beautiful and the trends more obvious. Hold on!

Key points

- Effective data use requires you to have good data literacy skills, be able to use and create data visualisations, and get to the point of data storytelling.
- There are two key groups of data that you will have access to in your organisation: qualitative (for example, text, open-ended, categorical data, ordinal data) and quantitative (numerical data, either discrete or continuous).
- Correlation and causation are different – two variables that have a correlation do not necessarily have a causation. It is important to know the difference – do not assume causation from correlation.
- There are many ways of categorising data. Commonly used data types include profit margins, customer preferences and customer demographic data.
- Triangulating data is when three or more data sets are used to identify trends, inform decision-making and guide action.

Triangulation makes decision-making and action more reliable as it is based on multiple sources rather than a single metric.

- Quantitative data can be considered as a point-in-time metric or viewed longitudinally. Both have an important role to play in business, as longitudinal data provides context and comparison.
- Thematic analysis is a process that can be used to analyse and interpret trends in qualitative responses. Qualitative responses are helpful because they provide detail that is lacking in quantitative data; however, analysing and using the data is time consuming.
- Knowing which data to chose or prioritise is a key part of the challenge of using data well. Following the six steps provided in this chapter could help you filter down the massive amounts of data into what is most important for you.
- Data plans are increasingly used in business to clarify and outline expectations of data use.

Reflection questions

- How would you rate your data literacy skills?
- How would you rate your data visualisation skills?
- How would you rate your data storytelling skills?
- What qualitative data do you have access to in your role? How do you use it?
- What quantitative data do you have access to in your role? How do you use it?
- Do you understand the difference between correlation and causation? If so, how would you explain it to your colleagues?

- Do you use triangulation in your role? Is there an opportunity for you to use this more in your work? If so, how?
- Of the data you use, how much of it would be point-in-time, and how much would be longitudinal? What do you find more useful? Is there a growth opportunity for you here?
- Do you use any form of thematic analysis in your work? Do you see this being a useful tool or something that is probably too much effort for the return?
- How do you prioritise the data that is used by you/your team?
- Follow the six steps of identifying data for your role or team. What came up for you throughout this process?
- Do you have a data plan? If so, is there any additional information that would be beneficial to include (i.e. columns)? If not, is it something that would benefit you/your team? Why/why not?

Chapter 3

Visualising data

> 'What paves the way for organisations to act on data is a framework where data is regularly communicated in the form of easy-to-understand insights.'
>
> (Sapirstein, n.d.)

Data visualisation is the process of putting 'data into forms we can see with our eyes' (Andrews, 2019). Data visualisations are powerful in using data to inform decisions – they make data beautiful by putting it into graphs, images or tables, meaning the trends are more easily identifiable and obvious. The old saying 'a picture is worth a thousand words' is particularly apt when we talk about data visualisations. Visualisations help show the trends without having to engage in significant cognitive load about the values themselves, and they truly can (and do) compress thousands of data points into one image. However, there is both a science and an art to developing effective visualisations (Knaflic, 2015).

Whatever your role in your organisation or the technology that you use, you must understand how to read and interpret the visualisations that you are given, *and* have the skills to create (or ask for) any additional visualisations that you need. No matter how good your technology solution is, the graphs it provides will never do absolutely everything that you need or want them to. There are times where you will need a custom-made solution to help you see the trends. The ability to read and create data visualisations are two of Ben Jones' (CEO of Data Literacy LLC) '17 key traits of data literacy'.

Why visualisations?

There is a lot of research available about the benefit of visualisations and their use in helping convey meaning. Road signs are a great example of the power of visuals. In Australia, kangaroos on roads can be a danger. Instead of filling a large sign with words explaining that there could be kangaroos on the road and to drive with caution, Australia's standards organisation created a yellow road sign with a picture of the kangaroo in the middle (figure 3.1). When I see this road sign, I know what it means. I don't have to read text to understand the possible risk to me as a driver, and to these beautiful animals. (Even writing that sentence required so much more cognitive load than almost instinctively responding to a single road sign.)

Professor Gillian Rose, who currently serves as Head of School at Oxford University, is a cultural geographer who has published extensively on visual mediums and the power of visual imagery. In her 2001 book *Visual Methodologies: An introduction to the interpretation of visual materials*, she said that of the five senses, vision is the most fundamental for many authors and researchers. Others suggest that this could be because 'depiction, picturing and seeing are ubiquitous features of the process by which most human beings come to know the world as it really is for them' (Fyfe & Law, 1988), and because 'seeing comes before words. The child looks and recognises before it can speak' (Berger, 1972).

Figure 3.1: Kangaroo road sign

This incredible power of visuals is partly because, as Rose (2001) suggests, they require the reader or consumer to consider their position in relation to the image. That is, they help organise information in a way that leads to us thinking and engaging with the information (Arnheim, 1969). As such, when employees, leaders, executives and board members see organisational data depicted visually, they are led to consider their role in, and the implication of, the visualisation for them and their work.

There has been a significant increase in the use of visuals in postmodern society (Rose, 2001), particularly in the technology-savvy and technology-full world that we now live in. In some ways, this is unsurprising – research indicates that of the information that our brain processes, up to 90 per cent is visual; the human brain can process an image in as little as 13 milliseconds; and people remember up to 80 per cent of what they see (Brown, 2018; Einsberg, 2014; iDashboards UK, 2018). It is not surprising, then, just how much people respond to visualisations of data rather than raw spreadsheets, in the same way that many of us prefer Instagram, TikTok and Zoom calls to texts and phone calls!

While visualisations are inherently useful and beneficial, there are challenges with creating good data visualisations – not all are created equally. You must seek to develop and use visualisations that help the information consumer interpret the data correctly (Rose, 2001). As statistician Edward Tufte said, 'for readers and viewers, the intellectual task remains constant regardless of the mode of evidence: to understand and to reason about the materials at hand, and to appraise their quality, relevance, and integrity' (2006).

When you're developing and producing visualisations, you may come across challenges around data manipulation, selectivity, how much information to include (visualisations that are too busy lose meaning and distract the viewer from the most important information) and complexity (complex visualisations can make the message unclear). If you are tasked with developing visualisations, you must aspire to develop good visualisations that support your work. You should consistently push yourself to consider the best type of visual and its characteristics, rather than reproducing the same thing that you have always done.

Reading the visualisations that you have

Before we talk about building your own visualisations, let's talk through what you already have available. There are many different technology platforms that your organisation may use to track and visualise data. Depending on the size of your business and your role in it, you might use tools for payroll and expenses, project management, website traffic and engagement, sales and point of sales information; or you might have custom-built solutions using products such as

Tableau or Power BI. Each platform collects slightly different data types, and visually represents the data in slightly different ways.

One of the questions I'm often asked in my role as a data storyteller is, 'Which technology and visualisation solution is best for an organisation?' Unfortunately, and perhaps frustratingly, there is no 'best' solution for all organisations – depending on your size, field, useful and important metrics, resources and access to technology, you will have different needs, even to businesses that you believe operate in a similar way to you. There are a lot of good technology solutions on the market, and there are a lot of ways that you can create and build a bespoke technology solution for your business. However, it really is a matter of establishing what you need and how you want the data presented and represented first, and exploring all of the options that are available.

Every visualisation that you are presented with on these platforms requires a level of understanding about them and what they represent. In chapter 2, we dug into the idea of data literacy and understanding the numbers – before you consider trying to read data visualisations, you need to understand the numbers and the context behind them. If you do not understand what the numbers mean, you will not be able to read or interpret visualisations accurately or reliably.

There is a different understanding and interpretation needed for each graph or visual you see. You might be used to seeing the following types of visualisations:

- line graphs
- bar graphs
- pie or donut graphs
- tables
- maps
- box plots.

Unless you have a basic understanding of visualisations due to being interested in data, or perhaps you remember what you learned in Year 9 maths, or you are curious enough to look up 'box plots' on YouTube, you may not have the skills or confidence to read the data in these different visualisations. The box plot is a common visualisation that I am often asked to explain – it might be used regularly, but many people do not understand what box plots represent or what they mean for them. (I'll talk more about box plots and how to interpret them later in this chapter.)

A challenge with using visualisations is the range of visualisations available on some platforms or dashboards, and the sheer overwhelm of not knowing what to prioritise or use. My friend Michael, who I talked about in the introduction, is a self-professed 'nerd' and is very good at organising and tracking his business results; however he admits that Google Analytics and all of the visualisations and options it contains has him completely stumped. He recently told me:

> 'There is just too much information in there. I don't know what I should be looking at or how to use it. I have data that shows me where my sales come from and the times that people access my site. But is that useful? Should I be paying attention to it? I know how to read it, but I don't even know whether it's important or not.'

Michael alluded to two key questions that many people have: what information in the visualisation is most important, and what should you be paying attention to? Unfortunately, the tools you have may not support this decision-making or help you engage at this level of analysis. Don't worry if this isn't currently one of your strengths – the next sections have some useful tips to help you work through these challenges.

Graphing 101

Before we start talking through the different types of visualisations that you have access to or might develop for yourself, there are a couple of things worth noting. Without an awareness of these factors, you could potentially misread or misunderstand a graphic – leading to incorrect assumptions, and decision-making that is not all that useful or accurate.

The first thing to be aware of is graph structure. Graphs often plot time across the page (on the horizontal/x-axis) and the metric along the vertical/y-axis. This type of graph represents how the metric has performed over time. The reason that time is usually on the horizontal axis is this axis should almost always have an *independent* variable on it – that is, something that generally continues, regardless of any other factors. Time continues regardless of what your business is doing, so it is usually independent.

The vertical axis usually shows a variable that is *dependent* on the other variable. For example, we talk about inflation as a percentage, so in an graph that represents inflation, the percentage is the vertical axis and time progresses along the horizontal axis. In a bar graph with categories and frequencies (such as the graphs depicting preferred cola brands we looked at in chapter 1), the horizontal axis is the types or categories being shown, and the vertical axis is the frequency of responses. This is because the number of people represented in each bar depends on the categories that are labelled on the horizontal axis.

Another factor worth being aware of is the way that graphs can be deliberately manipulated to exacerbate the appearance of differences, changes or consistent trends. In chapter 1 we saw, via the preferred cola brand graphs, how axis labels can be manipulated to make the data look better or worse. This type of manipulation can trick the viewer into believing the visual and jumping to conclusions, rather than thinking more deeply about the data itself.

The other factor to be mindful of is inconsistent increases in the scale or measurements on either axis. It is not easy to do this if you're creating graphs in spreadsheeting programs, but sometimes people do choose to design graphs to emphasise or minimise differences by changing the gaps or value size from one tick mark to the next. For example, if the axis begins at zero and increases in units of five, the axis should continue in units of five all the way along the axis, and each of the increments should be the same length on the axis. There should never be a change in the multiples as the graph progresses – for example, an increase in 5s that jumps to an increase in 15s. There should never be a change in the length between the tick marks, either – it should be consistent throughout.

If you notice issues with axis manipulation, it is important to identify the issue and then question why the person developing the visualisation wanted to manipulate the data in this way. You might want to go back to them and have them change or correct the axis. Being able to notice and recognise this issue is vital for being able to read and interpret data accurately. You need to be confident in not only identifying any issues, but asking questions as to why they might have come about.

Now let's take a look at some specific types of graphs you might come across, and how they can be read and interpreted.

Line graphs

Line graphs are probably very familiar to you, and it's usually quite straightforward to interpret and understand what the metrics are doing based on the trajectory of the line. Line graphs are particularly useful if you are interested in the performance or movement of a specific metric over time, such as revenue, profit margin or budget variation. Depending on the time period demonstrated on the horizontal axis, they can represent information in daily, weekly, monthly, quarterly, biannual or annual increments. There is no right or wrong unit of measurement – just what is right for the business and the metric. Share prices, for example, change every second, but different reporting mechanisms show summaries that show changes by the minute, and newspapers often report the closing price from the previous day.

If you have a premium LinkedIn subscription you might be familiar with the line graph that represents engagement with your profile over time. It is a useful representation because it shows the number of views that your profile has received each week and over the last three months, as well as other details. When you hover over a data point it reports on the percentage change in the number of views from the previous week, and the large number in the top left corner of the graph shows the total number of people who have viewed your profile in the last 90 days. This relatively simple visual representation outlines key metrics for people trying to build their positioning and exposure on the professional network. You could use this line graph to track how many people are viewing your profile each week, and see whether this is increasing or decreasing depending on the types of posts you are sharing.

Bar graphs

Bar graphs or charts are another common visualisation used to represent data; however, they are most appropriate when used for data that is discrete (that is, measured in whole numbers) or categorical (that is, there are categories to be represented) (Petkosek & Moroney, 2004). Bar graphs show the values or frequency of different elements in different columns, and the height of the bar represents the amount or value of the category. The higher the bars, the higher the frequency, and vice versa.

Bar graphs have a number of benefits, including: allowing the comparison of data across groups; show chunking or grouping bars in levels; and comparison to baseline information. However, they are sometimes overcomplicated with multiple bars for different measures or sub-metrics, and they lose their punch.

Box plots

If you are presented with a box plot like the example featured in figure 3.2 and you feel like you are out of your depth, don't worry – it would probably surprise you to know just how many C-suite executives I have worked with who have asked me to explain the box plot to them. Even though box plots are taught in middle school maths, it is often a long time between learning it in school and seeing one presented in a data visualisation tool or dashboard. Box plots are not commonly used on television or online news, and many of us are thrown when presented with one at work.

Figure 3.2: Example of box plots

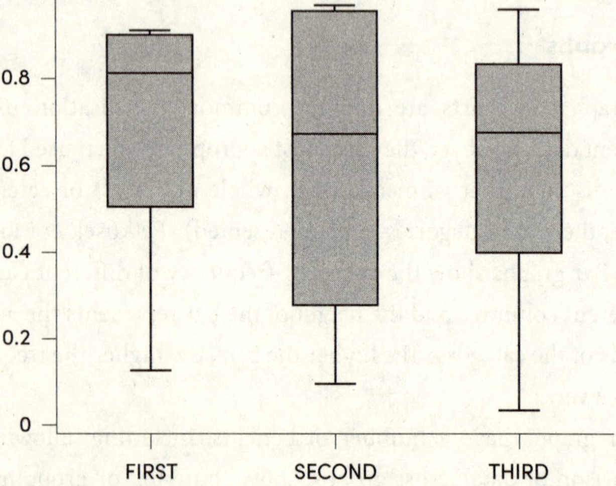

Box plots are really different to the previous graphs that I have discussed here. They were designed to show the spread of a data set, rather than the trajectory of a metric or frequency of a category. Each of the four sections (quadrants) of the box plot contain 25 per cent of the data. The spaces between the larger box and the two 'whiskers' on either end of the plot represent 25 per cent of the data (each), and each of the two boxes that make up the larger box in the centre also represent 25 per cent each. This never changes – it is always 25 per cent – so if a box or whisker quadrant looks shorter than the others, it means that the data is more compressed. Likewise, if the quadrant is longer, the data is more spread out. As mentioned in the introduction to this section, it is also important to remember that the middle point – that is, the horizontal line in the middle of the large box part – represents the median score; it is not the average/mean.

The average/mean score is calculated by adding up all the scores and dividing the answer by how many data points there were. This is often used in sport to represent an athlete's average batting score; when our smartphones show us our average amount of screen time each day in the last week; and when we hear about average fuel prices in our local area on the news. The median – represented by the horizontal line in box plots – is different. Think of it as the middle score – if all the data points were lined up in an ascending row, and you crossed off the first and last numbers continuously until you were left with one number, that is your median. The median is sometimes seen as a better metric to use than the average/mean, particularly if the metric you are looking at runs the risk of having a significant outlier or two. If there are outliers, these significantly different numbers have a considerable impact on the calculation of the average/mean, but they do not have the same impact on the median calculation as you are simply looking for the middle number. This is often the case with house prices, where the median is used so it is not skewed by exceptionally high or low uncharacteristic sales.

Just to confuse you, there is a possible spanner to throw in the works here. It will not always apply, as not all of the dashboards that might use a box plot visualisation will do this, but some will. If you see that your box plot looks like figure 3.2, this may not be relevant. However, if you have additional dots (as shown in figure 3.3), read on.

Figure 3.3: Example of box plots with outliers represented

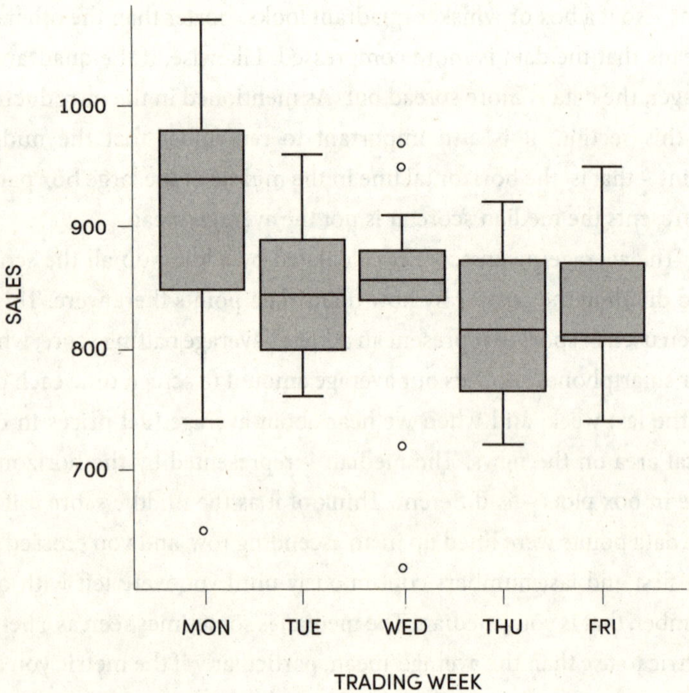

Some box plots show outliers. Outliers are results that differ significantly from the rest of the data set – that is, they are usually really high or really low. There is a mathematical way to work out whether a piece of data is an outlier, but you don't really need to know how to do this unless you are doing the calculations yourself (so feel free to skim over this part). If you are interested, to calculate the low point at which data becomes an outlier, the equation is:

Lower outlier cutoff = Quartile 1 − 1.5 × interquartile range

Similarly, to calculate the upper limit at which point data becomes an outlier, the equation is:

Upper outlier cutoff = Quartile 3 + 1.5 × interquartile range

Any data point that falls below the lower cutoff or above the upper cutoff is technically an outlier. But you will know whether the box plot you're looking at identifies them if you can see individual dots that sit outside the end of the whisker. Essentially, the person generating the box plot has chosen to represent the outliers as dots so that they do not alter the shape of the box plot representing the rest of the data.

Developing your own visualisations

The ability to develop your own visualisations for the types of questions you want to answer is a very useful skill. Visualisation platforms are great, but they don't always show you what you need to know or what is at the top of your list of priorities. Instead of trawling through spreadsheets and data sets, it is often quicker and easier to develop the visualisations you need so you can see the trends.

Take, for example, Claire Devine, artist and owner of The New Devine. She finds it frustrating that the software and products that she uses do not consider the clean split of income, expenses, living costs and wages, to give her an authentic and clear picture of her profit. She has had to do the work herself to ascertain the costs and percentages of each of these, and to visualise the information to help her plan for the future. Eventually she visualised her data and worked out that she needed to price her work at 4.2 times the 'cost' of production to cover her expenses and to make a profit. However, this information was not easily accessible nor visualised in the software. Claire now mentors other business owners who are new to small to medium business, and she shared that the people she has worked with have often focused on the graphs in business software that show income and expenses, or discussed their gross income. She said she actively works with them to organise, collect and visualise their data in a way that ensures their profit margin and mark-up are based on the numbers and percentage of costs and liabilities for their business.

Choosing the right visualisation for the metric you are looking at depends on several factors, many of which are discussed in the next section. There is a host of different design factors that will ultimately determine whether or not your visual 'lands' with the viewer. In her book *Storytelling with Data: A visualisation guide for business professionals* (2015), Cole Nussbaumer Knaflic outlines a six-step process for visualising and communicating data. The six steps are:

1. Understand the context.
2. Choose an appropriate display.
3. Eliminate clutter.
4. Draw attention where you want it.
5. Think like a designer.
6. Tell a story.

Within these steps, Knaflic (2015) outlines several challenges and potential solutions relating to graph design. Her recommendations include:

- Decluttering graphs to simplify the visual (removing all the graph elements that don't add to the message)

- Using bold, colour or boxes around text to highlight key information
- Using colour consistently and deliberately (using the same colours in similar graphs and presentations so the same colours mean the same thing, and being deliberate about the colours chosen for 'heat maps' and colour-coded data)
- Paying attention to the elements of the graph so there are clean vertical and horizontal lines (trying to order the data and the labels so it looks neat)
- Leveraging the power of white space.

As well as making good design decisions, it's also vital to have the technical skills required to build the graph or chart yourself. Not having the skills to do what you need in Microsoft Excel or Google Sheets is like owning a motorbike without a motorbike license; you can do some really cool stuff with it, but until you learn, its capabilities are completely wasted on you.

If you're trying to build your visualisation skills, there are plenty of places you can go to learn. There are Microsoft Excel and Google Sheets courses and tutorials, both paid and unpaid, which will assist in building your technical skills. There are micro-credentials available online, as well as plenty of free YouTube clips that unpack different skills. Find something that works for you, and commit to it. Like learning anything, it will be slow going to begin with, but you will get better at it, and you will get faster. Some of the key things you should look to upskill in (if you haven't already) are:

- data filters
- data sorting
- VLOOKUP formula
- COUNTIF formula

- SUMIF formula
- conditional formatting
- transposing data
- graphing.

It may not always feel as though you are making progress as you are building your spreadsheeting and graphing skills, but you will if you keep practising.

Which visualisation is best?

A question that I am often asked when I work with leaders is, 'Which is the best type of visualisation?' Again, unfortunately, there is no one best-fit visualisation out there. It depends on the type of data you are wanting to view and what you are trying to ascertain. The right graph is always 'whatever will be easiest for your audience to read' (Knaflic, 2015).

While there are no set rules about what to use and when, let's take a look at some handy hints that might be useful when you are choosing what to use to display your data.

If your data is categorical or discrete (for example, types of products, sales per country or income per customer) it is better (and technically more correct) to use a bar chart. Bar charts are a good fit for this type of data as each bar represents something that is quite separate and distinct to the bars on either side of it. A line graph is *not* the right option for this data, as line graphs should only be used where the data is continuous and each point on the line is connected to what is happening on either side.

The only time you should use a line graph is if your data is continuous – that is, there are no separate categories: one piece of data flows into the next in a continuous way. (If you are putting time on the horizontal axis, this is probably you.) Unfortunately, misuse of line graphs is a common issue. If you are looking at categories of data, you *must* use a bar graph.

If you're using a line graph, it's important to think about whether you need to adjust the vertical axis – not for the purpose of manipulating the data, of course, but to make it clearer. Also, think about the time period required across the horizontal axis. Remember, time will usually always be on the horizontal axis.

A pie chart is useful if you are showing the parts that make up a whole; however, there is a fair bit of widespread hate for this trusty little chart (which, in my opinion, is quite unjustified!). Historically, the pie chart has probably been overused, and 3D versions of pie charts are not good as they skew the view of different pieces; however, if you use this chart to represent a handful of elements that combine to make a whole it can work well, and it does serve a purpose.

If you're wanting to visualise a percentage score, or an average number (for example out of five), there are a couple of different options.

A fuel gauge indicates an overall amount or percentage out of the total amount available (see figure 3.4). This is useful if you are looking at the percentage for a single metric, or if you intend to show a couple of metrics side by side and would like to compare them.

Figure 3.4: Example of a fuel gauge

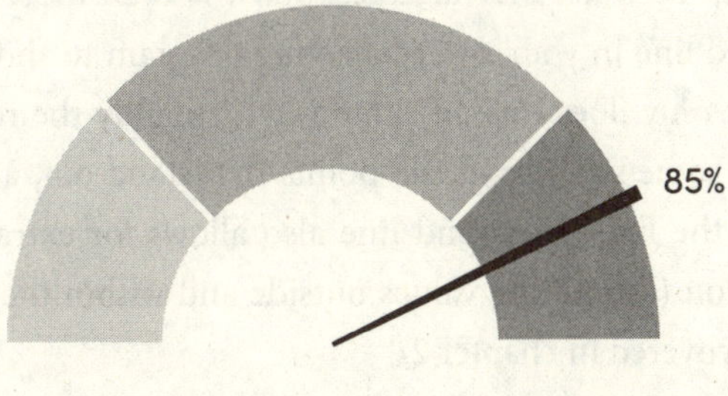

A bullet graph (figure 3.5) is quite similar to a fuel gauge, in that it's useful when you are comparing an overall score to a maximum value. When comparing data like this, it is often more useful to convert the data to a percentage, as the total or maximum number of the score could change. Percentages are always comparable.

Figure 3.5: Example of a bullet graph

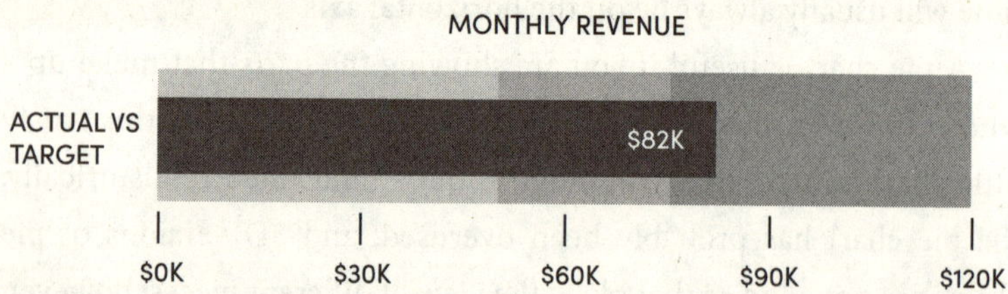

Lollipop charts (figure 3.6) are not used very often, but they are a really good way of showing the distance travelled from one point to another. If you are looking at a few different metrics side by side (or above one another) a lollipop chart allows you to see positive or negative movement and the size of the movement.

If you have two different variables and you are trying to look for a relationship between the two (for example, the relationship between the number of people who attend the beach on a given day and the daily temperature), the best way to represent this data is a scatter-plot (figure 3.7). A scatterplot positions dots on the graph for the combination of the data from the two points. It is useful to show the relationship between the variables, but it is even more useful if you add a trend line in your spreadsheeting program to show the overall trend. Not only does this, in some ways, simplify the relationship, it allows for some analysis of the points that stand out, and are a long way from the line. The trend line also allows for extrapolation and interpolation (estimating values outside and within the data values), which we covered in chapter 2.

Figure 3.6: Example of a lollipop chart

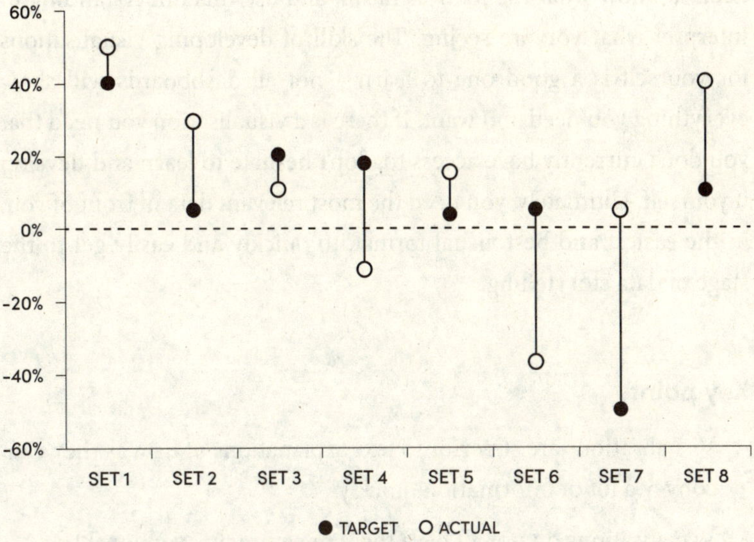

Figure 3.7: Example of a scatterplot

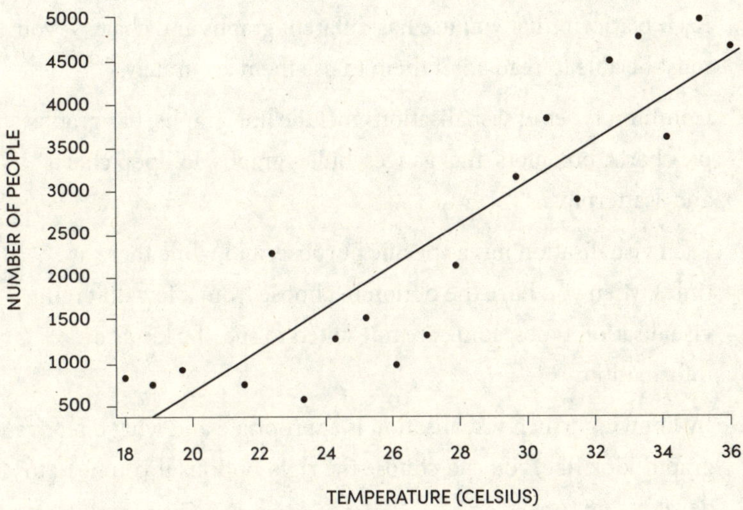

Regardless of the type of visualisations you choose to use, you first need to know what the metrics mean, and use this understanding to interpret what you are seeing. The skill of developing visualisations for yourself is a good one to learn – not all dashboards will show everything you need and want. If there is a visualisation you need that you don't currently have access to, don't hesitate to learn and develop it yourself. Ultimately, you need the most relevant data in front of you, in the easiest and best visual format, to quickly and easily get to the stage of data storytelling.

Key points

- Visualisations are superior to text explanations of data as they can convey a lot of information quickly.
- Visualisations do not all have the same efficacy – you must be conscious of developing good visualisations to ensure the data is interpreted accurately and the message is clear.
- You need to be able to read the visualisations that you are given. Each platform that you use has different graphs and charts – you must be able to read all of them to use them accurately.
- Common types of visualisations include line graphs, bar graphs, pie charts, box plots, fuel gauges, bullet graphs, lollipop charts and scatterplots.
- Each visualisation has a specific purpose, and while there are times when you have the option to choose from a few different visualisation types, some are not suited to specific kinds of information.
- By knowing which visualisation is appropriate and what effective graphs look like, you can choose the right options if you need to develop your own.

Reflection questions

- What visualisations do you have access to and use within your technology programs and platforms?
- What are the most useful visualisations for you, and why?
- What additional visualisations would support your work?
- How would you rate your skills in reading visualisations that you are given?
- How would you rate your skills in developing your own visualisations?
- What could enhance your skills in this area?
- Where could you get the additional help or support that you need?
- Can you explain the different uses of line graphs, bar graphs, box plots, lollipop charts and so on to others?
- What have you learned about developing effective visualisations that you can take with you into your work?

Reflection questions

Chapter 4

Establishing trends

> 'Data are not information; information is that which results from the interpretation of data.'
>
> (Mitroff & Sagasti, 1973)

One of the most important elements of effective data use is your ability to engage in data storytelling. Over the last few years, 'data storytelling has gained increasing importance as an effective means for communicating analytical insights to the target audience to support decision-making and improve business performance' (Daradkeh, 2021), despite the fact that it is an emerging field with limited empirical evidence. Data storytelling should always be the goal of using and engaging with data – if you don't think about the stories in the data, you have missed a significant opportunity and wasted a lot of time analysing data that won't have an impact. You might have exceptional skills in data literacy, a great understanding of the numbers, and be good at reading and interpreting the visualisations you are presented with and developing your own. However, all that time and effort is wasted if you are unable to, or you choose not to, engage in data storytelling.

Data storytelling is understanding what the numbers are telling you, and then communicating those trends and insights with your team to lead change where it is needed. It involves thinking about what the data is telling you about real people – that is, the impact of the data on real lives. It encourages you to think about your response to the trends you see. When you see these trends, you need to consider the way you communicate your insights to others – how you take key data to meetings, how you talk about it and how you highlight important elements or findings to your colleagues. How will you persuade others to see what you see, and the urgency that you see, in the data?

When I think about the importance of data storytelling, I think about the countless schools I have worked with that collect extensive data sets on attendance, standardised assessments, internal assessments, demographics, wellbeing, process and student perceptions – yet in so many instances, leaders and teachers tell me they don't know what to do with the data. You might spend a lot of time and effort collecting and visualising the data, but that doesn't mean it will make a situation better for the people in your organisation or your clients. Take, for example, Lisa, the CEO of a business school. She and her team had access to thousands of data points and visualisations for student engagement – she looked at them, she thought they were interesting, but until she started engaging in data storytelling, these figures and images did not shape her approach or focus, or direct her to specific actions.

There are two fundamental steps to data storytelling: first, you need to think about what the data tells you; second, once you know the trends, you need to think about how you respond. It's about looking for insights and trends in the data, being solutions-focused and then connecting the data to action. If all you do is look at the trends and think they are interesting, then file them away in a folder on your desktop, you haven't engaged in data storytelling – you only got part of the way there. As Brent Dykes – data storyteller extraordinaire – once explained to me, we need to move from the 'hmmm' moment of thinking something is interesting, to the 'aha' moment of shifting our understanding to what it means for us and what we can do differently.

The focus in data storytelling is on getting to the point of action. It can't just be about looking at the trends – it's how you respond that matters. Knowing that you lose, on average, 10 staff members per year means little unless you know whether the trend is increasing or decreasing, what portion of your staff this turnover is and *why* people are leaving your organisation. If people are leaving because they are genuinely being promoted and are moving on to better opportunities, this is confirmation that you need to keep doing what you are doing in developing your staff – it is obviously working. However, if your staff are leaving because they are unhappy, and exit interview responses are not as positive as you would like, data storytelling will allow you to build a narrative around this data, understand what the reality is and plan your action accordingly. Once you know these things, you can think about your response, what you need to do and how to build the culture in your team.

This chapter focuses on the first part of data storytelling – identifying the trends in the data – because it is not always easy to know what is important and what you should be paying attention to or using. Organisations have excessive amounts of data; you need to be able to sort through all the different movements in data and find the stuff that matters most. Chapter 5, focuses on the action that you take after you have identified the trends – that is, thinking about how you work with others to lead change and improve the situation for your employees, clients, customers or bottom line.

I am often asked for a specific formula for how to look at data, but like I have mentioned multiple times so far, there is no 'one size fits all' approach – there are many different needs for different people in different roles in different organisations. However, 'rules' aside, there are certainly some ways you can approach this process that will be more helpful than others. If you are closed off, fixated on one number, biased or trying to cover yourself, you will not engage in 'effective' or 'impactful' data storytelling. The following are five key principles that I have seen serve leaders well in the way that they approach data, and that have increased their success in data storytelling.

Principle #1: Recognise unique lenses

The first principle is to recognise that the things you notice and choose to highlight in the data will not be exactly the same as another person's analysis or storytelling. One reason for this is that we all come to the conversation with different experiences, skill levels and priorities, and we all have slightly different ways of seeing the world. Like in all aspects of our business, having these unique lenses and perspectives on the world enhances our work and encourages us to consider alternatives to our way of thinking. These unique views that people bring to the conversation are just as important for data storytelling.

The main thing to remember is that it is totally okay and normal for different people to identify, see and focus on different things in the data. Allowing people the time and space to share what they see might be a really important part of the process when you start to talk about trends, or do this work with others. It is also important to be mindful of this principle when you get to the stage of talking with others, or sharing insights with others, as they may not necessarily see the same thing you do. Be prepared!

The conversations that you have with your colleagues as you unpack and discuss the meaning of the trends and associated implications and actions are an important part of data storytelling. If you are looking for trends in a meeting with others, you don't have to see all the same things all of the time – it's the collaborative conversations and decision-making that emerge through the process that are valuable and will lead to transformational change (and we'll talk more about that in chapter 5).

Principle #2: Use multiple data sets

If you are seeking to find the golden nugget of the 'most important metric' or the 'one number that will tell us everything', the reality is that it is not likely to happen. You need to draw on multiple data sets to get a comprehensive picture of what is happening in your organisation. Even if your organisation focuses on a key metric like 'heads on beds' or 'on-time performance', you will need to have a broader and more comprehensive understanding of the numbers than just this factor.

There are many different types of data in your organisation, and depending on your role in it, the team you work in and your organisational priorities, different types of data will be useful at some times more than others. You need to be flexible in what you look at and when you look at it. Also, your team data priorities might be (and probably are) different to the larger goal of the broader organisation. For this reason, there may be other metrics that are more useful to you than the key or single business metric. Although the goal is to work towards improving the overall data or summary statistic, if you can't directly control it, it isn't useful for you to pursue it directly.

The notion of triangulation is also really important at all times when you are looking for trends in the data. As discussed in chapter 2, triangulation is when you consider three or more metrics to help identify trends – when you use multiple measures, you can trust what the majority of the data is saying. This process ensures that you are not making big decisions or acting on a single metric or measure, but are seeking similar, yet different information to confirm whether what you are seeing is actually a trend. Triangulation makes your findings and their associated actions more accurate and reliable, as they are based on a solid foundation of multiple data sets rather than only one.

Principle #3: Analyse data by zooming in and out

When you engage in data analysis and start to look for trends, there are several levels through which you can (and should) consider the data – again, it is not a 'one size fits all' approach. You can zoom out, take a broad overview of the situation and look at big summary metrics, or you can zoom in and look at more fine-grained and specific data. I often use the analogy of it being like taking a helicopter ride and flying over a town to get an overall view of the area, as opposed to what you see when you walk down a street looking at the detail of peoples' lives.

When you take a helicopter ride, you can see far and wide. You can take in the expanse underneath you, and experience that 'bird's eye view' of the world you are flying over. You see patterns in lines of streets and cars, and you identify similar characteristics in the homes and buildings you fly over, such as swimming pools or rooftops. If you fly near the coast, you can see the way the ocean wraps around the land and crashes into the rocks. It's beautiful, and it's a view you only get if you get in an aircraft and take a flight.

On the other hand, you can experience a town or city by walking or driving. You can go down different roads and laneways, you can see the cars in driveways and you can pat the dogs that you walk past in front yards. You can look at the houses that have been renovated, and marvel at old buildings that have stood the test of time and been preserved, despite all the years since they were built. If you are flying over a city, you can't possibly see the level of detail you get if you walk down the road and experience the specifics; but if you are only walking down the street, you can't get the broader, overall view of the town.

You need to have the skills and desire to look both from the helicopter view and the walk-down-the-street view. The helicopter view might tell you useful key indicators, such as the overall profit margin, annual turnover or percentage of revenue that your operating expenses or wages make up. However, this information is just a summary. It's useful, but it isn't the only way that you can, or should, investigate the data.

Since the helicopter view data points are a summary of the bigger picture, they are often an average. Averages can be helpful if you are going to use this statistic regularly or track the metric over time. However, as we learned in chapter 3, averages (means) do not necessarily give you small and tangible bits of information that you can act on. For example, if you look at the number of complaints that come into your business, you would be able to compare this number each month and try to reduce it over time. However, as you dig into the results, it becomes more useful for you to look at the departments, staff or business products that are receiving the highest level of complaints.

Averages and high-level statistics are useful, but they are fraught with danger as they mask a whole lot of detail sitting underneath them. Averages 'smooth out' the reality – they are a single point that represents a lot of data, and that data is potentially very spread out with some significant outliers. Averages lose the detail of the extremes, and don't necessarily show you what to do, or give specific details about the areas that need your attention. For example, if you are looking at your average billing per client, the average does not demonstrate that one big client engaged your services repeatedly during the year, or that another client only engaged you once, for a relatively minor service.

When you look at data through the walk-down-the-street lens, you break those big numbers and summary statistics into their smaller parts. Instead of looking at an overall profit margin, you might start to view trends in profit or turnover by geographical area, sales team, week or client demographics. Rather than only considering the number of new clients brought into the firm in the previous financial year, you might look at the highest payers, which staff have the highest billable hours, and those clients who take the longest to pay you.

A benefit of breaking down large data values into smaller parts is that you can understand more specific details about what is going on. You may not be able to directly impact the overall summary result, but you might be able to influence a couple of the parts of the whole. Breaking down summary statistics allows you to identify those outlying extremely high and extremely low results, and allows you to discuss and unpack why the results are so different. It lets you set small and measurable goals that you have a chance of achieving, rather than focusing on the big-ticket items that might be outside your direct sphere of influence.

Principle #4: Cut out the white noise

The goal of your analysis is to quickly, efficiently and accurately ascertain what data and which trends are important to you and your team. Think of yourself as the filter – when you are looking at the data, you are starting with a huge amount of information that could be fed into a funnel; your challenge is to identify the key data and the important messages so that you can use this information to make a difference.

Ultimately, you need to be discerning in your selection of the most important information, and the most important insights that you will use. You can't possibly utilise everything that is available to you, or take everything with you to a meeting, so you need to seek out the information that is not as useful, and filter it out. A key part of the next step of storytelling relies on you having actionable insights that you can communicate to, or decide on with, your team – so cutting out as much of the white noise as you can is a key principle that you should take into this activity.

A challenge that I often hear people face is the fear of missing something; this is a concern about risk. It is undeniable that if you cut out or omit the wrong piece of data at this point there could be significant consequences, depending on your role – so it is important to scan the environment, have a handle on the types of information that you have available and focus on the things that matter. Nobody wants to miss something they should have seen, ending up negatively impacting employees, customers or the company. You need to become discerning about the data that is useful and relevant for you, and focus on that. Developing a data plan first (as we discussed in chapter 2) might be a good way to start identifying what you need to be paying attention to.

Principle #5: Try to minimise errors in thinking

Regardless of how hard you try to minimise them, or perhaps even think they do not affect you, your cognitive biases impact the way you and members of your team think. Biases create unconscious errors in thinking and faulty judgement, and this leads you to misread or misunderstand the data and the trends. The important thing is that you are aware of them, you name them, and you actively seek to minimise the impact that they have on you and your team. The last thing you want is someone's bias leading you up the garden path!

Let's take a look at some of the most common biases that might affect your thinking when it comes to data.

Confirmation bias

Confirmation bias is 'the seeking or interpreting of evidence in ways that are partial to existing beliefs, expectations, or a hypothesis in hand' (Nickerson, 1998) and is 'perhaps the best known and most widely accepted notion of inferential error to come out of the literature on human reasoning' (Evans, 1989). American psychologist Raymond Nickerson stated that confirmation bias deserves more attention than the other problematic aspects of human reasoning. Confirmation bias causes you to select and focus on favourable information, or ignore unhelpful data, to confirm a hypothesis or a belief that you already have (Ruhl, 2020). You can see confirmation bias at work on social media, where people tend to create their own 'echo chambers' by following people who have similar views to them, as well as news sources and organisations that think about things in the same way. This indicates a broader challenge with confirmation bias, in that we tend to avoid actively seeking out sources and people who disagree with our views and perspectives (Ruhl, 2020), largely because it is easier and there is less conflict when we follow people with similar views.

This bias plays out whether you have a positive or negative belief or hypothesis. If you have a negative hypothesis or perception of what is going on with the data, you are likely to focus on the data points that confirm this narrative and ignore the positives, as they don't confirm your initial hypothesis. However, if you believe all is rosy and things are going well, you will tend to be drawn to, focus on and highlight the positive results, and ignore those that are negative – again, because the negative data does not confirm your initial hypothesis.

The example that I shared in chapter 1, where the CEO approached me to look over his 10 key indicators before he 'put a rocket up' his staff, was an example of confirmation bias. The CEO went into the analysis with the perception that not enough growth and progress had been made, so he focused on the data points that confirmed this narrative. Although more data points showed growth than decline (six out of 10), and the rates of growth were considerably higher than those that that were lower (approximately 10 to 15 per cent growth versus 0.5 to 1.2 per cent decline), he latched onto the data that confirmed what he thought. Thankfully he thought to involve me, and I had a more neutral view of the data.

Similarly, if a manufacturing company is focusing on growth and expansion, and its overall sales increased from the previous quarter, it is easy to focus on this single metric as confirmation that it is heading in the right direction. However, if other data indicate that expenses are up, delivery time has increased and customer satisfaction has dropped slightly, confirmation bias might lead the manager to ignore these other factors, and not seek out multiple measures of data to confirm the hypothesis.

One way to reduce confirmation bias's impact is to bring other people into the conversation, particularly people who are possibly more objective than you are, and also people who can offer other perspectives. Another is that, as Adam Grant (2021) said, we should all aim to think like scientists. When we think like a scientist (rather than a preacher, politician or prosecutor), we think about the data (and actively seek out the data) that does *not* prove the working hypothesis. By doing this, we are more likely to think about the alternate view, and we might be able to reduce confirmation bias's impact. A good way to think about this is to imagine someone was trying to argue the opposite case to what you have developed. What would they say?

Self-serving bias

Self-serving bias is another cognitive bias that can impact your work with data. Self-serving bias means that you tend to see positive results as a reflection of you and your efforts, but you explain poor results by blaming external factors (Ruhl, 2020). Shepperd et al. (2008) state that 'people view their positive outcomes as primarily internally caused, yet view their negative outcomes as primarily externally caused.' Examples include someone who attributes a promotion at work to their skill and effort, but limited opportunities for promotion to unfair or inequitable managers; or someone playing sport who attributes success to their personal contribution, but blames other external factors if they do not succeed (Shepperd et al., 2008).

Self-serving bias leads you to attribute the good news stories too heavily to your own contribution and role, rather than recognising the contribution of those around you. This can be very detrimental to your leadership. If a law firm celebrates significant increases in revenue in a financial year, the principal might too strongly attribute this success to their billable hours, effort or leadership of the team. This is a dangerous space to be in because, chances are, the entire team contributed to this success – not just the principal. If the leader doesn't adequately recognise the team members' contributions, this is a sure-fire way to reduce employee engagement and satisfaction.

Self-serving bias can also cause you to look at the negative or challenging data through the lens of blame and excuses, rather than taking personal responsibility for the outcome. This might cause you to blame external factors such as the market, the economy, the weather (!) or just bad luck, when potentially none of these things are to blame. When you're dismissive of the data in this way, it's almost the same as what Daniel Kahneman (2011) describes as a System 1 thinking response: you don't take the time to consider genuine reasons or solutions, but focus on jumping to conclusions to explain the reasons why something might have happened. (We'll talk more about Kahneman's work in chapter 5.)

Loss aversion

Loss aversion is another challenge with looking for trends in data. Loss aversion describes the tendency to prefer avoiding losses to acquiring equivalent gains. Kermer et al. (2006) provide a practical example of this: 'most people are unwilling to accept a 50-50 bet unless the amount they could win is roughly twice the amount they might lose.' It is not enough for the win amount to be equal to the loss amount; the gain has to be about twice as much.

Loss aversion is a particular challenge in organisational change, when leaders are forging forward with a change effort, or teams are tasked with making improvements. Because of loss aversion, people overemphasise the chance of loss, and weigh up the challenges versus what they have to gain.

I have seen this play out in a school setting, where there was a whole-school approach to improving students' writing results. The literacy results in standardised and system-wide assessments were low, and it was clear that improvements were needed so students were not disadvantaged. In a team meeting, where staff members were encouraged to think about how they might work to improve these results, many people were very hesitant. They focused on the potential losses (teaching time of the subject content, it being someone else's responsibility, not having the skills to teach writing), rather than the potential gains (students would perform better in the written tasks in their subject, and improving literacy was necessary for post-school life). Because many of the staff members did not deem the potential gains to be twice as significant as the potential losses, they were reluctant to make any changes to their practice; there was quite a bit of resistance to the proposed change efforts.

I saw a similar project unfold more positively in another school, where the leaders emphasised *why* they needed to focus on improving writing. Like Simon Sinek said (2009), the *why* grounded the educators in the bigger picture (outcomes for young people and post-school opportunities), and the focus was on preparing students as best they could to apply for jobs, write emails to their bosses and effectively engage in society. These teachers had some questions and concerns about how they would fit a new writing focus into their already significant workload, but the chance of positive outcomes for students felt much more significant than the potential challenges; therefore, they were largely on board and open to thinking about how they might do this better. It was a similar project to the previous example, yet the losses versus gains were framed and delivered in a very different way, and consequently the leaders experienced significantly different levels of employee buy-in.

Think about the ways that loss aversion plays out for you, and for people in your team. To minimise loss aversion's impact, the chance of success or positive outcomes needs to outweigh the negatives by almost double. This might be achieved by having staff buy in to your *why* – to have them understand the genuine reasons for the change, and the possible gains, rather than focusing on the negatives. When you can get this balance right, your change efforts are far more likely to be successful.

Fundamental attribution error

Fundamental attribution error is where people come to hasty conclusions about others who are responding to external factors, yet they don't do the same for themselves (Ross, 1977; Tetlock, 1985). When someone cuts you off when you're driving, you're likely to call them names or believe they are a bad person, whereas if you cut someone off, you excuse your own behaviour because you're running late or distracted by your kids. You treat the same situation differently, depending on where you fit in the story.

In some ways, fundamental attribution error probably sounds similar to self-serving bias, but the two thinking errors are, in fact, quite different. With self-serving bias, you attribute good news and results to yourself too heavily, and bad news to external factors. With fundamental attribution error, the internal and external are flipped, in that you excuse your poor choices because of external factors, but blame other people's internal or personality traits for their behaviour.

Fundamental attribution error happens in organisations in a few different ways. Most commonly, someone will attribute their colleague's poor performance to their personality, while blaming their own poor results on external factors that were out of their control. This is another way that the brain works against you: you attribute poor results to other people and assume it's about them as a person, but then jump to explanations and justification if you have underperformed.

Like the three previous errors in thinking, a good way to minimise fundamental attribution error's impact is to be aware of it, try to avoid it and provide additional opportunities to reconsider the information you have. It is important to note that these biases are not a type of deliberate data misuse, so they're different to what we discussed in the 'data misuse' section in chapter 1. Like all cognitive biases, these thinking errors are unconscious – they happen without you realising – and the unconscious nature of them makes it hard to identify when and where they have a negative impact. You need to be mindful of these biases, and seek to include others in your analysis, consider strategies for exploring other explanations and think beyond what your brain wants you to think as a first response.

If you're aware of the five principles outlined in this section and doing what you can to minimise potential challenges, you're far more likely to be successful in your use of data and evidence.

Establishing trends in the data

Establishing trends means looking for the nuggets of gold – the most important insights – from all of the data you have. Filtering countless types of data into insights is a slow, sometimes frustrating, yet deliberate process that you need to engage in. Cognitive psychologist Gary Klein suggested that insights occur when there is an unexpected shift in your understanding (Klein and Jarosz, 2011); and when it comes to using data, you are seeking that unexpected shift. Imagine you run a marketing campaign and you think it has been successful, but then you investigate the click rate, conversion rate and sales and find they are not as high as you hoped. If that shifts your understanding and you do something about it, it is an insight. Without a shift in understanding, you would potentially continue going about your work in the same way as you always have.

To get to the insights you're after, there are two different ways to approach the analysis: through an 'explanatory' or 'exploratory' lens (Knaflic, 2015, 2020). Researchers have used these two approaches for decades, and the clue to what the terms mean is in the names: explanatory analysis is where you seek evidence that explains something that you know or believe to be true, and exploratory analysis looks into a new phenomenon or looks to learn from the evidence collected. When it comes to using data in your analyses, you can take either approach; however, Knaflic (2015) suggests that when you are first looking at the data you are in the exploratory phase, and when you start to communicate with others you use an explanatory approach. She suggests that exploring is like opening 100 oysters to find two pearls, whereas you should only be sharing the pearls with your audience or team.

I agree with this sentiment, in that when you communicate with data, you need to be the filter that shows the audience the important parts, and not waste their time with the 98 oysters that don't have a pearl. But in the work I've done with teams across a range of organisational fields, the way I see people use 'exploratory' and 'explanatory' analyses is actually in the way they approach the task to begin with. If a team has a hunch that their customer wait time is too long, they could do an explanatory analysis that allows them to dig into all the data related to this specific problem in an attempt to explain the phenomenon. They wouldn't necessarily look at other, unrelated data, just the customer experience metrics. They could use this information as a team to discuss how they could address and improve customer experience. If a business owner has a goal of increasing production by 20 per cent, they could do an exploratory analysis to investigate capacity and current usage of different machinery, current levels of (and therefore how to optimise) logistics involved in the process, and the profit margin of increased production. With this data, they could make informed decisions about where to focus their attention and plan steps to lead change.

Both scenarios are the right way to go about the problem, and both exploratory and explanatory analyses have a time and place.

So when it comes to the practicalities of *how* to establish trends, keep this in mind. Are you digging into the data to test a hypothesis, or explain or provide more detail about a hunch that you have? Or are you looking at a particular goal or focus area and trying to ascertain and explore what is going on?

Either way, the following guidelines might be useful to direct and order your thinking throughout the process. As mentioned previously, it is not necessarily possible to create a step-by-step guide for you to use every single time you attempt to engage in analysing data, but these general and broad guidelines might be useful in some instances. (In saying that though, feel free to rethink the way this could be done and adapt it to fit your context.)

1. Decide whether you are engaging in an exploratory or explanatory analysis. Are you looking to explore and learn more about a particular area of your business or goal area in your organisation? If so, you are doing an exploratory analysis. Or are you trying to test a hypothesis or look into a hunch that you have? This is an explanatory analysis.
2. Regardless of whether you are doing an exploratory or explanatory analysis, you need be able to cut through the huge amounts of data you have so you can focus on the data that really matters to you and your team. The data that is most important to you is the data that is going to help provide relevant information about the area you are investigating. If you have a data plan, it could be a useful document to support this process, or you could go through the six-step process in chapter 2 to identify the data types that are most useful for you.
3. Refresh your thinking on the five fundamental data principles I explained earlier in this chapter. Remind yourself of the ways that you will approach this analysis and the things that you will be mindful of. If you are looking for trends in the data with your team, make sure you share these principles with them, and agree as a team to actively use the principles and commit to working together to do the best job you can.
4. For each piece of data that you are looking at, you will need to think about how you can zoom in and out (helicopter view versus walking down the street) and establish what is best suited for each data set.
5. Once you have the appropriate level of 'zoom' established, ask yourself some or all of the following questions for each of the sets of data. As you are doing so, take notes on the things you notice and the things that stand out to you:
   - Generally, what is the data doing (increasing, decreasing, being inconsistent/no trend is obvious, or staying the same)?

- Are there any data points that surprise you or stand out? Why? Why do you think the data could be like this? What do you think it is telling you?
- What are some positives that you see in the data?
- What are some areas of growth in the data that you are viewing?
- What does the other data that relates to this aspect tell you? Use the above questions as you look at this data, too.
- Given what you can see across multiple data sets, what are some possible suggestions or opportunities for you, your team or your organisation?

6. With the list of things that you have identified in the previous step, place the observations into the Eisenhower Matrix pictured in table 4.1 (Covey, 2004). This requires you to decide whether the trends are urgent or not urgent, and important or not important. Combined, each of the trends that you see will fit into one of the four boxes in the matrix.

Table 4.1: Eisenhower Matrix

	Urgent	Not urgent
Important		
Not important		

7. Once you have put all your trend observations into the Eisenhower Matrix, review their position and move them around until you are happy that they are in the right spot. If you are involving your team, do this task individually first, then create one master Eisenhower Matrix that you all agree on. This will take time, as you will have a range of observations and you may not all agree on the appropriate quadrant to begin with, but stick with it until you have a version that everyone can agree on.

While this process will not help you with *what* to do, it will hopefully get you into the stage of thinking about what you see, and which of those trends are more important and urgent than others.

Additional analysis questions

In the previous section I gave you some broad questions about general trends that can start you thinking about what you see and what is important. This list was a short sample of possible questions – your analysis will look different depending on the role you are in and what you are looking at. I encourage you to add your own questions.

In a previous book that I wrote for teachers, I developed a more comprehensive list of questions that could be useful when looking for trends in data. Although I wrote them for educators, they are just as applicable here, and consequently I have adapted some of them to share with you. The idea is *not* that you start from the top and work your way to the bottom. Instead, you should choose a handful of questions that you think would be useful to use in your analysis and focus on those only.

The questions are:

- What do I notice about the data?
- What is it telling me?

- What do I wonder about the data?
- What is it measuring?
- Is it reliable data?
- When was the data collected?
- Who collected the data?
- What is the purpose of the data?
- What questions do I have about the data?
- Who do I need to approach to find out the answers to these questions?
- What does the data tell me about individual/team/organisational achievement?
- What does the data tell me about individual/team/organisational progress?
- What are the outliers?
- Why do these anomalies exist?
- Is there any data that doesn't make sense?
- Why doesn't it make sense?
- Are there any immediately identifiable trends in the data? How do I know they are trends?
- Which individuals/subsets of the data have high results? How do I know they are good results (what evidence is there)?
- What is most remarkable about the data?
- What areas of the data can I celebrate?
- Which individuals/subsets of the data have performed poorly? How do I know they are poor results (what evidence is there)?
- What areas need my attention?
- Is there a 'middle group' of data? What does this represent? How do I know this?
- Is the data similar to previous results? Or is it an improvement/ does it show a decline? What does this tell me about products/ approach/marketing/(insert your focus area here)? Are longitudinal comparisons available?

- What does the data tell me?
- What does the data *not* tell me?

(Used with permission. Adapted from *Using and analysing data in Australian schools* by Selena Fisk. ©2019 by Hawker Brownlow Education, hbe.com.au. All rights reserved.)

In this chapter, we've explored the idea of data storytelling principles, and I provided some starting guidelines for establishing trends in the data. Principles guide you and your use of data to tell stories, as there is no 'one size fits all' approach to data storytelling. Guidelines, on the other hand, are slightly more concrete processes of the ways that you can look at the data, rather than the lens through which you see it. Both principles and guidelines outlined in this chapter could be useful for you to use as an individual, or with members of your team. No matter how good your data literacy and visualisations, unless you get to the point of data storytelling you are significantly underutilising the bucketloads of data at your disposal, and missing an opportunity to make a real difference.

Key points

- Data storytelling should be your goal – if you don't get to the point of storytelling, the data won't impact your organisation, clients, employees or outcomes.
- You need to be able to identify trends in the data, and prioritise key information that you need to address and share with others.
- There are five fundamental principles that you should remember when you are engaging in data storytelling: recognise unique lenses, use multiple data sets, analyse by zooming in and out, cut out the white noise, and try to minimise errors in thinking.

- Confirmation bias is 'the seeking or interpreting of evidence in ways that are partial to existing beliefs, expectations, or a hypothesis in hand' (Nickerson, 1998).
- Self-serving bias is when 'people view their positive outcomes as primarily internally caused, yet view their negative outcomes as primarily externally caused' (Shepperd et al., 2008).
- Loss aversion is the idea that if provided with a choice, the perception of a loss far outweighs the perception of a gain, by a ratio of approximately 2:1 (Kahneman et al., 1991).
- Fundamental attribution error is where people make personal inferences and hasty conclusions about people who are responding to external factors (Ross, 1977; Tetlock, 1985).
- There is a series of guidelines as to how you might approach the data to identify important and urgent trends. This process could be used by yourself, or with your team.
- Think about the questions that will best serve your purpose, organisation and team. Choose the most useful and relevant questions from the list provided, or adapt and create your own.

Reflection questions

- How would you rate your skill in data storytelling?
- What are your skills like in knowing which data to pay attention to?
- What data do you pay attention to the most in your role/organisation? How do you know that this is the most important information for you?
- In your data storytelling, how does 'recognising unique lenses' impact your work or team?

- In your data storytelling, how does 'use multiple data sets' impact your work or team?
- In your data storytelling, how does 'analyse by zooming in and out' impact your work or team?
- In your data storytelling, how does 'cut out the white noise' impact your work or team?
- In your data storytelling, how does 'try to minimise errors in thinking' impact your work or team?
- Out of confirmation bias, self-serving bias, loss aversion and fundamental attribution error, what do you think is the biggest challenge for you? What do you see as the biggest challenge for people you work with? How do you discuss this with members of your team?
- How would you adapt the six-step guidelines to work for you and your team? How can you best tailor it to suit your needs?
- Which of the analysis questions work best for you or your team/ context?
- Which analysis questions would you use, and for what purpose?
- Which analysis questions are not useful for your context?

Chapter 5

Making decisions and taking action

'The ultimate purpose of taking data is to provide a basis for action or a recommendation for action.'

(Deming, 1942)

Once you understand the data, utilise visualisations, have a strategy for narrowing your focus and have identified the key trends, the next step is to engage in storytelling so the data and your insights can have an impact. This means you need to start thinking about actions, and making decisions.

There are two important things to consider when you talk about your insights with others. The first is how you will communicate the data and its messages. This is vital – you must use language and tone effectively to persuade your audience to buy in to the urgency the trends illustrate and motivate them to progress the conversation to action. The second consideration is the action you will take and decisions you will make as a result of the trends that you see. You must be future-focused and solutions-oriented. You might engage in this process yourself, or with your team – either way, the process and thinking are the same. Unfortunately, humans are great at making plans and having goals, but not great at the execution (Covey et al., 2012). This chapter will unpack both talking about data with others, and how to make good decisions and take action.

Task #1: Discussing data

When you convey messages about the data to others, it is important to be mindful of the way you 'speak data', so that you communicate important insights effectively – especially to non-technical audiences (Daradkeh, 2021). Many people find this a challenge; but given the way we learned language and maths in school, and how separate the two tended to be, it's understandable that we don't know how to tell stories with numbers or that it doesn't come naturally (Knaflic, 2015).

The way that we communicate is a key element of data storytelling. This is where you consider how you share the insights that you have gleaned with members of your team or board. The skill may not come naturally to you, or you may not have had much practice with it yet, but that's okay – there are some key things you can learn about the language that you choose and the way you speak about data that will help you communicate effectively.

Brent Dykes, author of *Effective Data Storytelling: How to drive change with data, narrative, and visuals* (2019), developed a useful Venn diagram to convey the elements that he believes must be present when telling good 'data stories'. You can view Brent's model on his website at effectivedatastorytelling.com.

Dykes' Venn diagram consists of three overlapping circles. In the first circle, at the bottom, is *data*. You need to know what the data is saying, and you need to include it and talk explicitly about the data in your data storytelling. In the second circle, on the top right, is *visuals*. Like kids' picture books, visuals that complement a story help convey meaning and enhance the audience's understanding of what is going on. In data storytelling, visuals do the exact same thing; however, as discussed in chapter 3, you need to be deliberate and discerning about the visuals that you choose to use. In the third circle, on the top left, is *narrative*. Just like we get better at reading stories to kids, Dykes said, we can get better at building the narrative of our data stories with practice over time.

The most interesting part of Dykes' model, I think, is the overlap of the sections of the Venn diagram. If you can use *data* and *visuals* together, he suggests you will (only) *enlighten* your audience. Enlightening your audience means that they see the data and the visuals, but do not have a story that is associated with either part. If you use only *data* and *narrative* together, you will *explain* what is occurring. However, without the visuals, you could lose meaning or emphasis, and miss the opportunity to capitalise on the power of visuals in the narrative. And when *narrative* and *visuals* only are combined, the audience will be *engaged* – but there is no hard data or specifics to motivate the audience or pinpoint the challenge. However, when you can overlap *narrative*, *visuals* and *data* in your communication, Dykes says you can lead *change* (pictured in the centre of the Venn diagram).

Think for a moment about a presentation you have seen that you considered to be an effective data storytelling exercise. What worked well in that presentation? Chances are, if it was effective and memorable it would have included the three elements that Brent mentions – a narrative that talked you through the trends, some visuals to display the trends, and the data itself. On the flip side, think about a time you have witnessed a presentation you would NOT consider to be effective data storytelling. What went wrong? What was the presenter missing?

When I work with executives and leaders, I deliberately seek to combine the three elements in Dykes' model into my presentations – so I have experienced the benefit of doing so first-hand. While I was writing this book, I presented on data storytelling to a group of leaders. At the beginning of my presentation I shared a story that highlighted the impact they could have on individuals. In doing so, I showed a visual, discussed the data and talked specifically about one person and his data – his name was Luke. About five hours later, when I was wrapping up the workshop, one of the participants came to me and talked through a challenge she had. She said that it was a similar example to the one I talked about with Luke. What surprised me most was not only that she connected with the specific story I told, but that she took on the message and explained the similarities and differences between Luke's story and her team. She referred to Luke by name – she wanted to have an impact on the 'Lukes' that she worked with! Pretty powerful stuff.

Tone and language choices

The tone with which you speak about data will have a significant impact on whether or not your message lands with your audience. Think about an impassioned speech that you have heard. Martin Luther King's 'I have a dream' speech and Winston Churchill's 'We shall fight on the beaches' speech are remembered today not only because of the content and the turning point in history, but for the passionate and persuasive manner in which the speeches were delivered. If you live in Australia you will probably have seen footage of Julia Gillard's 'misogyny' speech in federal parliament. She nailed the content, but her delivery – the pauses, her tone and her passion – is why it stands out as a key moment in Australian political history.

Your delivery – and the genuine interest and passion you have for leading positive change – will directly impact the way others engage with your data storytelling. If you're trying to influence those around you, you need to control your delivery – you can tone it up or down, depending on where you and your audience are with the data. I have seen leaders motivate and inspire their teams to engage with the data because they are passionate, they have been able to articulate why they are engaging in the work and they actively build others' capacity and want to bring them along on the journey. I have also seen leaders who have failed miserably in their attempt to engage in data storytelling with others. It's usually because they have treated it as a compliance activity, and this message has been conveyed to their audience when they have discussed it.

The worst thing you can do when you are talking about data is to say you are doing something because 'the board' or 'the CEO' wants you to. Simon Sinek (2009) said we don't inspire people through compliance – we need to tap into the broader organisational goals, the positive impact and the influence others can have to really engage them in the process. Ultimately, 'compliance programs don't normally prioritise the need for strong employee engagement, but without it your compliance efforts can quickly breakdown' (Human Resources Today, 2020). Rigorous and authentic engagement in data storytelling will not be achieved unless you are able to motivate and engage your colleagues in the process, and your choice of language and your tone are key factors in this engagement.

The power of the narrative

Data storytelling is a complex skill. A key element of being able to demonstrate this skill effectively is in the inclusion and development of the narrative, which is a significant focus of much of the existing literature on data storytelling (Daradkeh, 2021; Dykes, 2019; Knaflic, 2015; Vora, 2019). Just like you can approach the initial analysis from an exploratory or explanatory lens, there are different types of data stories that you can tell. Vora (2019) identified four common types of data stories: reporting stories, decision stories, probing stories and pitching stories. Reporting stories provide information or updates on what has happened; in decision stories, the audience relies on the storyteller to help them tell the story and make a decision; probing stories are more exploratory in nature, helping others look for or at potential opportunities; and pitching stories are those where data is used to pitch and justify a new idea or approach.

Depending on the purpose or type of data story that you are telling, there are different structures that the story could follow. Some of the most commonly known and used story frameworks are Aristotle's tragedy structure (a beginning, middle and end); Freytag's Pyramid (an exposition/introduction, rising action, climax, falling action and dénouement/conclusion); and Campbell's Hero's Journey (17 stages that are in three main elements: the departure, initiation and return) (Dykes, 2019; Knaflic, 2020).

While these are fiction story structures, data narratives can be developed using any one of these storytelling frameworks. They have stood the test of time with fiction works; they have captivated audiences through a range of film, television and print media; and they are effective because they build tension and ultimately impact the viewer's thinking. There is no single best way to tell a story or a simple way to characterise the way a story must be told (Knaflic, 2020), but you can look to the research to give you some ideas on the best ways to go about it.

Dykes (2019) proposed a modification of Freytag's pyramid, which he called the 'data storytelling arc'. His model includes four steps:

1. **Setting:** the background (including the hook)
2. **Rising insights:** digging further into data that is the focus of your data story
3. **'Aha' moment:** the story's climax or central insight
4. **Solution and next steps:** actions and recommendations.

This modified process, as Klein and Jarosz (2011) suggested, is constructed to lead the audience to the point where they have an unexpected shift in their understanding, which means they are more likely to actually do something about the insight.

In their book *Switch: How to change things when change is hard* (2011), Dan and Chip Heath talked about some of the challenges in leading change. They said leading change is like leading an elephant and a rider down a path. The rider is more logical and facts-based, whereas the elephant is more emotional. The rider needs to be able to control the elephant, but it is much smaller in stature and weight! This analogy of the elephant and rider is useful in the discussion on how to tell good stories; it's a reminder that you need to not only speak to the rider (rationally) but motivate the elephant (through feeling) to get them to do what you want them to do.

When you were a student you would have liked some teachers more than others. There might have been a subject that you initially disliked, but the teacher really got you into it and you didn't hate it by the end. The truth is that the teacher you loved so much probably didn't teach you anything different to the teacher next door – schools generally all work from the same curriculum, and teachers in the same subject in the same year level usually have to teach the same stuff. But it was the *way* that they taught that you connected with. You probably don't even remember the content they taught you (unless there was a really cool science experiment) but you do remember them. And they were able to get you to buy into the subject.

That is your job when you are telling data stories. Facts alone might appeal to a small number of statisticians or Excel whizzes in the room, but you need everyone on board. To do that, you have to provide data but also motivate the elephant with feeling. You must connect your data to true stories and real lives, talk about the impact and potential that you see, and celebrate the growth and improvement that has already happened. Don't fall into the trap of thinking that it is all about the numbers – it actually isn't!

Disappointing data

One of the challenges in communicating insights and trends is when the data doesn't tell you what your audience wants to hear. This is particularly awkward if you're charged with sharing the insights with the team, but you know that it is not what your C-suite executives or board want to know or were expecting to hear. Although in theory it is easy to say 'better the devil you know', the reality is that you can never completely anticipate what the best way to deliver the information is, or how your audience will react. Your audience might have worked really long and hard on the particular product or offering that you need to talk about, so it is understandable that it hurts to get feedback that their work has been ineffective.

Despite how uncomfortable you might feel about sharing the 'disappointing data' with others, you need to lean into the discomfort – as Dr Brené Brown (2012) said – and share this message with your team. Patrick Lencioni (2021) talked about leaders having the responsibility to, at times, be a 'little j' jerk (rather than a 'big J' Jerk) – the former being the bearer of honest, sometimes confronting, yet necessary news; the latter being someone who is deliberately mean. You have a professional responsibility to be the 'little j' jerk, take the disappointing data to your team and avoid sugar-coating it. You can't bury your head in the sand and hope things will get better, or think you can distract your audience with other data. If it is important and urgent, you *must* take it to your team.

As well as it being the right thing to do ethically, executives and board members have a greater legal responsibility than ever to address and act on data they are provided with – particularly data that demonstrates risk, error, health concerns or misconduct. In many parts of the world, executives and board members are increasingly being held personally liable for accidents and crises when there is deemed to be enough evidence that the person was aware, and chose not to act. Executives and board members can be sued for being 'negligent' if they have ignored the evidence and potential risk that exists in their organisation.

In Australia in 2014, there was accident where faulty brakes on a truck led to the death of a 56-year-old trucker, Robert Brimson (Hancock, 2015). The CEO of the trucking company, Peter Colbert, was jailed for 12.5 years for manslaughter because he didn't act on warnings that the truck had faulty breaks. The court felt that Colbert had been given the information on the issues with the truck and its maintenance history, and had deliberately not acted. His decision to not take action was deemed to have endangered Brimson's life, ultimately leading to his death. This is just one example, but there are increasingly more stories emerging like this, where senior executives and board members are held personally responsible for failings with in their organisations.

In the US, the seminal criminal negligence case of *United States v Park* (1975) 421 US 658 led to development of the 'Park Doctrine', which holds people responsible if they are in a position to know and correct issues with food safety. Mr Park was the CEO of a food chain, and he was convicted of storing food in an area that was prone to rodents, ignoring a previous health mandate. Subsequent trials often use this case as precedent, due to the finding that corporations could be held criminally accountable for wrongdoings – even if it was not intentional or deliberate misconduct.

As a key insights gatekeeper, sharing the right data must be a greater priority than your fear of having difficult conversations. You must seek to be truthful and transparent about the data you find. When you are truthful, you tell the story as you see it and as it needs to be told; when you are transparent, you don't hold back or filter your insights – you share the things you need to share when they need to be shared. You have an ethical and legal obligation to do so.

Task #2: Solutions-oriented decisions

While it is incredibly important to get the tone, language and content of your data messaging right, the next significant task that you have is to think about how you will respond to the trends. You might be engaging in this process by yourself, or you might be having this conversation with others in your sphere of influence. Either way, the outcome of the analysis and unpacking of data should always be about solutions, focusing on what you should do next.

The Stockdale Paradox

In his book *Good to Great: Why some companies make the leap... and others don't* (2001), Jim Collins talked about organisations that have experienced significant challenges and slumps in performance, productivity or sales, yet been able to turn this around to become great companies. He discussed how leaders in these 'good-to-great' companies responded to the challenges in front of them, while also having an unwavering faith that things would get better in the future. When it comes to being solutions-focused in your approach to data, like Jim Collins said, you need to face your current challenges while staying focused on your long-term aspirations.

Collins called this notion of duality – of holding both your current reality and future aspirations – the Stockdale Paradox. The name comes from Admiral Jim Stockdale, who was in the Hanoi Hilton – a prisoner-of-war camp during the Vietnam War. He was imprisoned from 1965 to 1973 and tortured more than 20 times during this period. When Collins met Stockdale, he asked how he was able to survive, despite all of the terrible things that were happening to him. Stockdale told Collins that he stayed focused on the end goal, hoping that one day he would return home.

When Collins asked about the types of people who didn't make it out, Stockdale reported that it was 'the optimists'. Collins was confused – how was being optimistic different to Stockdale hoping that he would return home one day? Stockdale replied that the optimists were always hoping they'd be out by a certain date – they'd be out by Christmas, then Easter, then Thanksgiving. When each holiday passed and their hopes came to nothing, they died 'of a broken heart'. Stockdale said:

> 'You must never confuse faith that you will prevail in the end – which you can never afford to lose – with the discipline to confront the most brutal facts of your current reality, whatever they might be.'
>
> (Collins, 2001)

For people in this situation, the ability to hold the current reality in one hand while staying committed to the future aspiration was the deciding factor. Collins connected this story to several organisations that he had worked with, and noted that when trying to improve, companies should also aim to confront the challenge in front of them, as well as holding onto the aspiration of future improvement (Collins, 2001).

I think the Stockdale Paradox is a helpful theory. If you are facing a challenge, wanting to make a change or undergoing a review, it is important to deeply understand your current reality, face what is in front of you and seek to make it better. However, you also need to hold on to the end game – to keep in mind the larger aspirations and goals that you have, and never lose faith in achieving those goals.

I recently worked with a Chief Information Offer (CIO) and a team of healthcare professionals. The CIO's long-term goal was for everyone in her team to be able to understand the organisational data they were given, to enhance the overall quality of healthcare they were providing in their different health facilities under their broader organisational umbrella. However, there was a lot of data, and some important trends that needed to be acted upon by people at a range of levels in the company. When we first spoke, she said that data was seen as the job of the 'analysts', or those people who have 'data' in their job descriptions; health professionals preferred to think about patients and their individual health data, rather than broader organisational trends. Her goal was to build individual team members' skills so they could more thoroughly understand the organisation's numbers, do the data storytelling at a strategic level, and engage in conversations about the trends and possible responses.

Her goal was to enhance the quality of healthcare, but she also needed to think about the current skill set in her team, and what was needed to support her staff to move towards this point of enhanced practice. Over time, we planned out an 18-month program of building middle managers' skills. This included a self-reflection tool for all participants at the outset, and the program evolved as different employees showed growth, struggled with some elements and moved more quickly through others. We provided time and space for them to learn, explore and make mistakes, and to share different interpretations of what they saw and what they thought it might mean. Slowly but surely, we saw improvements in their interpretations, they began to ask better questions and they started to think about actions, and then lead change in their own teams. We faced the challenges directly in front of us, with the middle managers, while staying focused on the overall goal. The overall patient satisfaction rating went from a 3.8 out of 5 to a 4.6 out of 5, and the CIO felt that it was largely due to having a large goal to aspire to, while facing the reality of her team's skill set at the time.

Slow and deliberate thinking

Nobel Prize winner and Israeli economist and psychologist Daniel Kahneman's work in his book *Thinking, Fast and Slow* (2011) is also really useful. Kahneman identified two main systems of thinking – System 1 and System 2 – which have very different purposes, and pros and cons, and show up at different times.

System 1 thinking is fast and automatic, and there is very little cognitive load that goes into thinking this quickly. System 1 serves a purpose, because you don't need to think deeply about every little decision you make. If you are asked if you would like a coffee, or if you would 'like fries with that', you don't need to engage in deep, deliberate, considerate thinking where you weigh up your options, consider other points of view, think about possible answers and then make a decision. Our System 1 thinking brain engages with the question and quickly knows that it is a 'yes' to coffee and a 'no' to fries. Kahneman found that, on average, we use System 1 thinking about 98 per cent of the time!

On the other hand, System 2 thinking is slow and deliberate. It's the conscious engagement you have when you think about solutions, explore ideas and uncover new possibilities. It's beneficial when you're problem solving, thinking about a challenging problem or brainstorming all of the possible options. If you have a disagreement with someone you care about, you think deeply and slowly about how you could respond, how you might reach out or whether you should send the first message. That thinking is slow, measured and deliberate, and it helps you evolve and grow. The harsh comments you make during the disagreement are definitely a result of your System 1 thinking taking over!

We all use System 1 and System 2 thinking in different degrees. I'm sure you can think of someone who makes a lot of rushed decisions, and someone else who seems to take forever to think through all the possible options.

Both System 1 and System 2 thinking are ever-present in data conversations, and the pros and cons of each have an impact on the way people respond to data. System 1 thinking is evident when people make quick judgements or justifications of results, rather than engaging in thinking about all the possible explanations. I worked with a group of real estate agents recently, and there were some people in the room who jumped to blaming markets and interest rates and didn't want to engage in a conversation about other gaps; they didn't want to think deeply about what the numbers meant. We engage System 2 thinking when we think slowly about data.

I recently worked with a not-for-profit organisation that had a high staff turnover, and the leadership team genuinely wanted to understand the employee experience and think about possible options for enhancing employee engagement to boost retention. We spent a lot of time looking at the types of employee data they had, considered other ways of engaging employee satisfaction data, and thought about how to get feedback from staff as they were leaving and from those who were still in the organisation. They brainstormed ideas and developed a plan of action as a result of this discussion, which included practices that recognised and celebrated achievements and milestones, provided scope for employees to determine their own professional learning, and reviewed systems that gave staff more regular feedback. Although this work is in its infancy at the time of writing, initial feedback has been positive and no-one else has left for a sideways job offer. System 2 thinking was vital for this project to have its intended impact.

In his book *How to Make the World Add Up: Ten rules for thinking differently about numbers* (2020) Tim Harford talked about the usefulness of Kahneman's framework when thinking about numbers. He adapted the framework of fast and slow thinking to the notion of fast statistics and slow statistics. He said fast statistics are those that come quickly – they are immediate, and they are powerful. Slow statistics are a thoughtful, unbiased collection of information. Harford talked about news reports, and the ways that we are often drawn in with fast statistics (like 'red wine reduces the chance of heart disease'), but we need to think more slowly and deliberately about the data (because, yes, in some instances, red wine might reduce the chance of heart disease – but not in every human, and not in all quantities).

System 1 thinking and fast statistics will rarely help you or the people you work with – even if it's the first logical explanation that emerges, and requires minimal effort (Shepperd et al., 2008). You must think about how you can drag yourself and your team members back into the space of System 2 thinking. You want people thinking slowly and deliberately, not jumping to the first, hasty conclusion that pops into their mind.

One way to do this is to notice the first thing that comes to mind (whether it be a reason for a trend or a possible solution) and then sit and wait. Challenge yourself/others to think of a second reason or possible solution, and then a third. Give yourself the time and space to think more slowly about the data, and know that your brain wants the decision-making to be done quickly because it wants an easy solution.

One of the activities I do with teams is to have every member of the group silently brainstorm a minimum of nine reasons for, or solutions to, the trend they see. I have everyone write down their nine reasons or solutions individually, and I don't let anyone share until everyone has all nine. Once everyone has their list, I spend time talking through all of the ideas that each person wrote down, and we have an open discussion as a group. I have found this process to be really useful (even for myself when I am thinking about ways to respond to a challenge) because it is relatively easy to come up with a couple of quick solutions, but they are not necessarily the best options. It is not easy to fill the nine boxes, but by putting these parameters in place and giving time for thinking, it is a great way to force System 2 thinking, and explore possible options that may not have come to you otherwise. It is a great way to think outside the box and beyond what your System 1 brain wants you to do.

Think again

In chapter 4, I briefly introduced organisational psychologist Adam Grant's work in *Think Again: The power of knowing what you don't know* (2021). Grant said we should be aiming to continually evolve and develop our thinking, and never hold onto an idea (or, in this case, a solution or action) too tightly as the 'be all and end all'. Our thinking and decision-making should advance and be rethought as we gain new evidence and insights.

In his book, Grant stated that people think in one of four ways: like a politician, a prosecutor, a preacher or a scientist. A politician is someone who seeks the audience's approval, or sticks to a message they believe in. A preacher thinks they are inherently right, and tries to sell the message to others or persuade others into thinking the same way that they do. In prosecutor mode, a person tries to prove that they are right and the other person is wrong. However, in all three of these thinking styles, the person's views and perceptions are fixed and do not change, regardless of the evidence that is presented to them.

Instead, Grant suggested that we should aspire to think like a scientist, where we treat our knowledge and thinking as though it is not fixed. Thinking like a scientist involves testing out ideas, floating hypotheses, collecting information, and shifting perspectives and thinking according to new information that we find along the way. Not only do scientists look for data that proves them right, but they actively seek out data that proves them wrong. Generally, scientists are okay with this because it is more important that they get it right rather than being right themselves. This is similar to the approach that Dr Brené Brown takes with her work, including on her podcasts *Unlocking Us* and *Dare to Lead* – where she repeatedly said she is 'here to get it right, not to be right'.

In business, the idea of thinking like a scientist can be challenging, as you may not always have the time and space to create and test hypotheses, collect data, reflect on the impact that the processes have and make adjustments. When profit margins are the bottom line, sometimes this dominates your focus, and does not allow for trying new things – because what if you get it wrong? However, it is possible (and encouraged) to treat your evolution as an individual and a member of a team or organisation as through you are working through an action research cycle.

If this is a daunting prospect, think about starting small – explore the ways that you could enact an inquiry cycle on employee satisfaction, customer engagement or staff retention (something that isn't as big as the profit margin!) so that you can build an understanding of what is happening before tackling bigger challenges. I have seen (and worked with) plenty of employees and middle and senior managers who have been apprehensive about an inquiry process, but who have started small and given it a go. Inevitably, they have an impact, which is professionally rewarding and confirmation that they can make a difference. I encourage you to challenge yourself to think like a scientist – who knows what you might find out, and what you might learn along the way!

Thinking about action

The Stockdale Paradox, thinking slowly and rethinking with new evidence can all help guide your and your team's work in data storytelling – and help you avoid falling into the thinking traps I covered in chapter 4. If you think any of these theories are particularly useful for your team, share a summary with your team members prior to beginning the data conversation. Talk explicitly about the things that will and won't work for the team. Lean into the vulnerability of having this conversation. If you're comfortable, you might even think about sharing with your team what you personally struggle with the most.

In the section 'Establishing trends in the data' in chapter 4, I proposed a series of seven guidelines to help you cut through the noise of the data and visualisations you have, so you can find the trends that are worth noticing, sharing and acting upon. Given you are now at the stage of communicating and sharing these trends with others, there are additional guidelines that can be added to the end of this process:

8. Once you have your trends and insights outlined in the Eisenhower Matrix (see table 4.1 in chapter 4), work out the order in which you will address them by numbering each quadrant of the matrix as follows:
   1. Important and urgent
   2. Important but not urgent
   3. Urgent but not important
   4. Not urgent and not important.

9. Start with quadrant 1 (important and urgent). Write down why each of the trends and insights is there. What made you categorise it as urgent? What made you think it was important? What is the goal of being able to act on this particular trend?
10. Once you have a good understanding of why your trends and insights are urgent and important, think about the additional information that you will need for the discussions that you will have about the data:
    - What additional visuals do you need use to convey the key meanings that you have derived from the data?
    - When you explain the trends and what you see to others, what metaphors and specific stories will you use to tell the story and build the narrative?
    - How will you explain the possibilities and opportunities?
    - What language will you use so that your suggestions are more likely to be well received?
    - How can you be deliberate in your tone and messaging so that you are priming the audience to receive the information well and be constructive in their response?
    - What is the narrative that you will develop around the data to convey meaning and to be persuasive?
11. Complete the 'nine solutions' exercise I mentioned earlier in this chapter – where each person silently brainstorms nine possible solutions or responses that you could take to address the trends. (You can do this with your team, or individually.)
12. Position each of the nine actions in one of the four quadrants in the effort versus impact matrix (table 5.1).
13. Depending on how far you want to go (and how many actions you have listed), repeat these steps for the 'important but not urgent' and 'urgent but not important' insights in your Eisenhower Matrix (table 4.1).

14. Whether by yourself or with your team, develop a plan for the actions in the following order:
    - Cross out (or delegate if you really want to) the 'low effort, low impact' actions – you don't want to waste time on these things when they won't have much impact.
    - Tackle the 'low effort, high impact' actions first, as they will be quick wins that will build momentum and encourage you and your team to keep going.
    - Where possible, delay (or even ignore) the 'high effort, low impact' activities. Invest this time instead into the actions that will have a greater impact.
    - Invest resources (time and finances) into engaging in the actions that are 'high effort, high impact'. These will often be your longer-term projects that will involve multiple staff/teams.

Table 5.1: Effort versus impact matrix

Low effort and low impact	Low effort and high impact
High effort and low impact	High effort and high impact

While you're going through these steps, it is important to ask good questions of the data and the trends, so that you are finding out everything that you need to, and therefore acting and responding appropriately. While there are some questions provided above to prompt you, it can be useful to plan out a few key questions that you would like to use or focus on that will illicit the necessary reflections on the data and have you thinking about action, prior to engaging in this process. In chapter 4, when I talked about looking for trends in the data, I suggested starting with broad set questions about general trends, and then becoming more specific as your skill and that of your team increases. It is the same for focusing on actions – you can be really broad and generic to begin with, particularly if you or your team members are new to these types of conversations, but increasingly be more specific and narrow in your focus as your skill improves.

Like in chapter 4, there are some additional questions proposed below that you might find useful throughout this process. As with the previous set, these questions are not to be done in order, or all of them at the same time. It is best to choose a couple of questions that work for you and your context (maybe two or three) and focus on those. Feel free to adapt and rework the questions as you become more confident and proficient at this process. Here are the questions:

- What are some possible reasons for the results?
- What does the data tell me about the current products/approaches/strategy?
- How do I know this is a reflection of the products/approaches (what evidence is there)?
- What specifically needs to change as a result of this data?
- How can it inform practice/decision-making/process?
- What are the next steps?
- Why does it need to change?
- Who will benefit from the change?
- What specifically will I do to make this change?
- What is the timeline for this change?
- What will I do if there is no improvement in the future?
- When will I measure this data again?
- How will I know that this change has been successful?

- How can I use this data to celebrate success/achievement with my team/with others?
- How can I use this data in feedback with and for employees?

(Used with permission. Adapted from *Using and analysing data in Australian schools* by Selena Fisk.

Once you have answers to these questions, you will need a clearly defined plan of action that you can use to lead the shifts you are chasing. In their book *The 4 Disciplines of Execution: Achieving your wildly important goals* (2012), Covey et al. explained that acting on and being responsive to the information we have and the plans we make is, often, the hardest part – the part where many of us fall down. Their '4DX' model includes four key steps in executing plans:

1. Focusing on the 'wildly important goal' (WIG)
2. Acting on lead measures (which you can control, rather than lag measures, which you can't)
3. Keeping a compelling scorecard to keep people, teams and the organisation on track
4. Creating a cadence of accountability.

Breaking down your goals into manageable tasks that you and your team members can take ownership of, and experience some success with, is the best way of changing habits and practices. Putting in place processes to check in with your and others' progress towards the goal will keep everyone accountable and moving forwards.

Leaning into data conversations

The previous steps provide some guidance on the order in which you might approach an analysis, either by yourself or with your team.

The guidelines provide a useful framework from which to organise your thinking and progress you along the journey.

However, if you are doing this work with teams, the way in which you manage and lead this process is vitally important. Just like the tone and language discussed in task #1 earlier in this chapter, you need to be deliberate in the way that you approach, outline and run the meetings in which data is discussed. You want people to engage in the process, be constructive in their contributions and discussions and, ultimately, build their skills – this is how you'll incorporate data storytelling into the organisational culture. Remember, it isn't just the 'data people' who own or use data – we all need to be building our skills and those of others.

If you are new to this and haven't yet led any conversations about data, I encourage you to push through any apprehension you might be feeling and give it a go. Like any new skill, the more practice you get with data storytelling, the better you will be. There will be a steep learning curve at the beginning, and you will have to be really deliberate and conscious of all your decisions and all the language you use, but it will get easier and feel more natural over time. There is also no end point to learning the skill of data storytelling – as data evolves, your understanding evolves, you learn new things and we will all improve.

If you do want some pointers on how to introduce data storytelling in a team meeting, the following guidance might be useful. Note that you may want to do this process first as a reflection activity just for yourself, before you take it to your team.

First, set aside a meeting time to discuss the data. Make it clear that you will be discussing a key section of your organisation's data, and consider sharing the data beforehand so your team members know what you will be discussing. Giving people an opportunity to see the data before they arrive at the meeting allows them to undertake some of their own analysis and form their own opinions beforehand, rather than being put on the spot in the meeting. Providing the data ahead of time lets people start to unpack it on their own terms, and has the potential to alleviate some of your team members' concerns – particularly if they are worried about whether they will have the skills to engage in the conversation.

Lead the conversation by sharing your 'why' for the use of data and what your goals are. Remember, your 'why' is not accountability or compliance. Explicitly connect and explain your use of data with your own vision (or the organisation's vision), and emphasise the role it will play in understanding your work, your clients and your impact. When you are able to recognise and connect data use with your 'why' and your broader purpose, you are much more likely to motivate and inspire your team to view the data through the same lens.

Be honest with your team about your current skill level. This might be confronting, but that is okay. As Dr Brené Brown (2009) said, lean into the discomfort and your own vulnerability by acknowledging that you are new to this work, and that you don't have all the answers. At the same time, also publicly recognise that data-informed decision-making is best when it is collaborative, as we all see and interpret data in different ways. Normalise that there are no silly questions, that you are collectively learning together, and that you will all evolve and learn at your own pace – and that's okay.

Ascertain your team's level of comfort and views on data. Perhaps start by getting them to explore their position on a scale of one to 10 for how useful they believe data is, and their skill in using data. Ask them where they would rank themselves individually, and the score they would give the team as a whole. It can be useful to follow up down the track to see if anyone has changed their perspective or ranking as a result of their learning or progress.

Begin talking about the data by asking broad inquiry questions to begin with. You could even start with very basic questions such as 'what do you notice?' or 'what questions do you have?'. These broad questions are less daunting than targeted questions, and are a great entry point for people starting to talk about data. As the group's skill increases and people become more comfortable with the process, you can be more specific and targeted in your questioning, and even encourage others to create their own questions.

You will probably have to spend a lot of your initial meetings in the data literacy and data visualisation space so everyone understands what data they have, what it means and how to interpret the visuals. Spend whatever time you need explaining the metrics, unpacking the visualisations and talking through trends. Without this understanding, you can't expect your team to be able to engage with the data in a constructive and accurate manner.

As skill and understanding improves, think about how you can move into the space of data storytelling. Start by asking your team:

- What is the data telling us?
- Now that we know this, how can we respond?

Be really specific in your actions and plan out the steps. Think about who will do what and by when, and how often you will come back together to check in on your progress.

Talking about the data and making evidence-informed decisions is a huge step forward. It can also be a significant challenge, particularly if you have not engaged in this type of work before. This chapter has focused on being future-focused and solutions-oriented with your data, once you have identified what is urgent and important for you and your team. When you're in team situations, you need to be able to discuss the data in a way that promotes positive and critical thinking and reflection – and you can do that by being deliberate about your language, tone and manner. Plenty of the data that you come across in your work is interesting, but nothing will change until you put in a concerted effort to grow and adapt your practices – and those of your team.

Key points

- When you make decisions with data, you need to consider two key elements of working with others: how you will discuss data with your team (your tone, language and manner), and how you can lead colleagues into making good, solutions-oriented decisions.
- Communicating disappointing data – that is, trends, outcomes or results that are lower than, or different to, what you had hoped or expected – is a challenge. You need to lean into honesty and transparency to build trust. Despite the discomfort of having these conversations, you have an ethical, and often legal, responsibility to do so.
- The Stockdale Paradox describes people and organisations that are able to address the current reality they face and respond to the challenges in front of them, while also having an unwavering faith in achieving the overall goal. This is an important skill when engaging in data storytelling.
- Daniel Kahneman developed the idea of System 1 and System 2 thinking. System 1 is fast and has limited cognitive load; System 2 is slow and deliberate. You need to harness System 2 thinking as much as you can when you're using data and evidence, and actively build the conditions for you and others that encourage slow and deliberate thinking.

- Adam Grant proposed four types of thinking: thinking like a prosecutor, politician, preacher or scientist. Only when you think like a scientist can you adjust your thinking and take in new information, test out hypotheses and learn and adapt as you go.
- This chapter expanded the series of guidelines from the previous chapter to include how to talk about data and engage in decision-making. Guidelines such as these support the process, and are particularly useful if you are new to this or unsure how to lead these conversations.
- Leading the process and others in meetings is not necessarily an easy task – again, this is particularly so if you are not overly comfortable talking about data. I've given suggestions of things you can do in your meetings to actively build a culture where people are open and willing to talk about data.

Reflection questions

- In which area are you stronger – how you speak about data, or how you mobilise others to engage in constructive, solutions-oriented actions?
- What challenges do you have in talking about data or leading data conversations with others?
- What concerns do you have about discussing challenging trends or data? What have you seen others do (both good and bad) that you could learn from?
- What are your thoughts on the Stockdale Paradox? How do you focus on your current reality and face immediate challenges while keeping your eye on the ultimate goal?

- What is your default thinking system – System 1 or 2? How can you encourage yourself to be pulled into System 2 thinking? If you believe your default is System 2 thinking, how can you foster similar deep reflection and thinking in others?
- What is your most common type of thinking – prosecutor, politician, preacher or scientist? How can you prioritise your use of scientific thinking and hypothesis testing?
- Do you ever treat your work like an inquiry cycle, or action research cycle? Why or why not? What opportunities are there for you/your team?
- What are your go-to strategies for communicating data to others? What can you focus on or spend more time on?
- What tools have been helpful in thinking about the way you frame, plan and execute the meetings where you talk about data?

Conclusion

> 'I'm a very serious "possibilist". That's something I made up. It means someone who neither hopes without reason, nor fears without reason, someone who constantly resists the overdramatic worldview. As a possibilist, I see all this progress, and it fills me with conviction and hope that further progress is possible. This is not optimistic. It is having a clear and reasonable idea about how things are.'
>
> (Rosling, 2018)

Regardless of the job you're in, there's an increasing expectation that you understand what data means, what it is telling you and how you should respond. Data is no longer the responsibility of the official 'data people' in our organisations – we all need to be able to read, engage with and think critically about the numbers that we have. As these expectations are increasing, so too is the number of data sets and types of data that flood our businesses. We don't even need or ask for much of the additional data we're given – it's just added to the huge lists we already have. This leads to further noise and confusion.

At the beginning of this book, I shared the story of Michael, my tech-head buddy who, despite wanting to learn and make the best decisions for his business, struggles with the huge amounts of data he is given. As I was coming towards the end of writing this book, about four months after I first interviewed Michael, I received an email from him with the subject line: 'This is exactly what I am talking about'. Michael had an advertisement running on Google for his photography business, and Google sent through an email that asked him to click a button to automatically apply the 21 recommendations it had. The recommendations included:

- enhanced CPC
- target ROAS
- add DSA
- raise CPA target
- set CPA target
- target impression share
- broad match for fully automated conversion-based bidding
- keyword deduping.

As a small business owner, Michael is trying to do his best – but as he said to me in his email, he doesn't know what any of this means or what he is doing. There are so many options and things that could be enhanced in his advertisement, but it's a struggle to understand any of it. Sure, he could pay someone to manage his advertisements for him and maximise their return (which he may need to do if he wants to expand), but in the meantime, he is inundated with additional data that he doesn't know how to use. The message here, and the reminder to you, is that you are not alone if you don't understand the numbers and analytics.

In the introduction to this book, I shared the six levels of skill in using evidence to impact your work. Take a look back to figure 0.1, and consider which category you now belong to. I hope that by reading this book, you have progressed up these levels towards the place of reflective practice. As you learn more, build your skills, begin to ask questions of the data and engage in data storytelling, you can move from being an unconscious user, to conscious, to using data casually, to having an awareness, to taking action and to engaging in reflective practice.

I have lost count of the number of people who, in my work with teams, executives and individuals, have said to me, 'Oh, Selena, but I'm not a numbers person.' I don't believe your skill level is fixed, or that you 'are' or 'are not' a numbers person. Depending on your background, previous training, the type of role you're in and the expectations of your organisation, colleagues and team, you fit somewhere on a 'numbers person continuum'. You move up and down the continuum when you practise (or don't), and I have seen people move considerably up the continuum from starting at a low level. My experience has shown me this, and I wrote this book because I know it is possible. Finding numbers easy and enjoyable to work with is undoubtedly useful and makes the work easier, but even if this isn't your natural state you can get there.

For me, a numbers person is someone who understands the metrics, can read what they are given (and maybe even develop some of their own visualisations), and looks for trends in the data. They have skills in communicating the data to others. They have conversations about action that are future-focused and solutions-oriented. They act on what they see, and take steps to rectify and adjust things that are not going well. They think slowly and critically about the information they are given; they regularly reflect on the actions they have taken; and they celebrate success with others when the data improves. Numbers people are inherently just people who enjoy seeing evidence of their impact, and knowing they are making a difference.

You now have all you need so you can be a numbers person, too.

Glossary

Anecdotal data. Information that is not in numerical form and is usually not recorded or written down. It's evidence and information that you see and learn from along the way.

Causation. One step further from correlation – it is where you definitively see a connection or relationship between two variables (one thing is known to cause another).

Categorical data. Qualitative data that is put into categories. Common examples are grouping data by state or territory, or broad categories of product type.

Continuous data. Numerical, quantitative data that continues and can (almost) take any value within the range. Continuous data often (but not always) contains decimals, and numbers can move up or down in small, incremental amounts.

Correlation. Two variables have a correlation when there are trends or patterns in the way the variables behave. Correlations can be strong or weak, and positive or negative. Correlation does not mean that one thing causes another.

Data literacy. Good data literacy is understanding what the numbers mean and the context around them, and having (at least) a basic understanding of how they are calculated. You need to understand the numbers and their meaning to be able to use and engage with them effectively.

Data storytelling. The goal of effective data use. To get to the point of data storytelling, you need to know what the data is saying (what the trends are), know how to communicate the insights with others, and think about how you will act or respond to the trends.

Data visualisation. Data that is presented in graphs, tables or other images to make the trends easier to identify, and to reduce the cognitive load of engaging with extensive sets or lists of raw data.

Discrete data. Numerical, quantitative data that is not continuous. It exists (generally) only in whole numbers – such as the number of employees, clients or product lines.

Key performance indicators (KPIs). The key elements or metrics identified in your organisation that you are aiming for or working towards. For example, targeting a number of new clients or guests, or setting sales targets.

Longitudinal data. The same data set tracked and compared over time.

Ordinal data. Qualitative data that is grouped into ordered sets – for example, 'strongly agree' to 'strongly disagree' survey questions.

Percentage. The proportion of something, relative to the whole amount. Percentages are often more useful to compare different data points, as they allow for fluctuations in value and provide a more accurate comparison.

Point-in-time data. A single metric or a set of data that represents one snapshot of time.

Profit. The amount of money earned, once costs have been removed. Should be expressed in dollar value.

Profit margin. The proportion of earnings that are profit. Profit margin is calculated by dividing the profit (in dollars) by the revenue, then converting the result to a percentage.

Qualitative data. Data that is generally text-based or category-based. It provides more detail and explanation of a phenomenon than quantitative (numerical) data, but it is more difficult and time consuming to analyse. An example is the comment written on a Google review (after you have given a quantitative score out of five).

Quantitative data. Data that is numerical. It is easier to analyse than qualitative data as it can be easily summarised, visualised and compared. However, it lacks the detail and explanation of qualitative data. An example is a rating score out of five for a Google review.

Revenue. The money generated by your business, whether that be sales, operations, royalties or other fees. Sometimes called 'turnover'.

Summary statistics. Overall summary data that represents the spread or central tendency of the data set. Mean, median, mode, range, interquartile range and standard deviation are examples of summary statistics (Hand, 2008).

Triangulation. Using three or more data sets to consider trends in the data. If the data is varied, trust what the majority of the data is telling you. Triangulation is more reliable than trusting or relying on only one data source.

References

Amini, F, Brehmer, M, Bolduan, G, Elmer, C & Wiederkehr, B (2018). Evaluating data-driven stories and storytelling tools. In N. Riche, C. Hurter, N. Diakopoulos & S. Carpendale (Eds.), *Data-driven storytelling* (pp. 249–286). A K Peters/CRC Press.

Andrews, RJ (2019). *Info we Trust: How to inspire the world with data.* Wiley.

Arnheim, R (1969). *Visual Thinking.* University of California Press.

Australian Bureau of Statistics (n.d). 'Statistical language – Correlation and causation.' abs.gov.au/websitedbs/D3310114.nsf/home/statistical+language+-+correlation+and+causation.

Berger, J (1972). *Ways of Seeing.* Penguin Books.

Braun, V & Clarke, V (2006). 'Using thematic analysis in psychology.' *Qualitative Research in Psychology,* 3(2), 77–101.

Bridgwater, A (2018). 'The 13 types of data.' *Forbes.* forbes.com/sites/adrianbridgwater/2018/07/05/the-13-types-of-data/?sh=6a2ef5423362.

Brinton, W (1914). *Graphic Methods for Presenting Facts.* The Engineering Magazine Company.

Brown, B (2012). *Daring Greatly: How the courage to be vulnerable transforms the way we live, love, parent, and lead.* Penguin.

Brown, S (2018, 19 Jul). 'What is the impact of visual content marketing?' Rocketium. rocketium.com/academy/impact-visual-content-marketing.

Busby, A (2019, 4 Mar). 'New PwC survey reveals consumer data is the most highly valued.' *Forbes.* forbes.com/sites/andrewbusby/2019/03/04/new-pwc-survey-reveals-consumer-data-is-the-most-highly-valued.

Colangelo, S (Director) (2020). *Worth* [Film]. Netflix.

Collins, J (2001). *Good to Great: Why some companies make the leap… and others don't.* Random House.

Covey, S, McChesney, C & Huling, J (2012). *The 4 Disciplines of Execution: Achieving your wildly important goals.* Simon and Schuster.

Covey, SR (2004). *The 7 Habits of Highly Effective People: Powerful lessons in personal change.* Simon and Schuster.

Daradkeh, MK (2021). 'An empirical examination of the relationship between data storytelling competency and business performance: The mediating role of decision-making quality.' *Journal of Organizational and End User Computing (JOEUC), 33*(5), 42–73.

Deming, WE (1942). 'On a classification of the problems of statistical inference.' *Journal of the American Statistical Association, 37*(218), 173–185.

Desjardins, J (2019, 17 Apr). 'How much data is generated each day?' World Economic Forum. weforum.org/agenda/2019/04/how-much-data-is-generated-each-day-cf4bddf29f.

Dowker, A, Sarkar, A & Looi, CY (2016). 'Mathematics anxiety: What have we learned in 60 years?' *Frontiers in Psychology, 7*(508).

Dykes, B (2019). *Effective Data Storytelling: How to drive change with data, narrative and visuals.* John Wiley & Sons.

Einsberg, H (2014, 15 Sep). 'Humans process visual data better.' Thermopylae Sciences + Technology. t-sciences.com/news/humans-process-visual-data-better.

Evans, JSBT (1989). *Bias in Human Reasoning: Causes and consequences.* Lawrence Erlbaum Associates, Inc.

Feinberg, KR (2006). *What is Life Worth? The unprecedented effort to compensate the victims of 9/11.* Hachette.

Fisk, S (2019). *Using and Analysing Data in Australian Schools.* Hawker Brownlow Education.

Fisk, S (2020). *Leading Data-Informed Change in Schools.* Hawker Brownlow Education.

Fyfe, G & Law, J (1988). *Picturing Power.* Routeledge.

Gallo, A (2016). 'A refresher on statistical significance.' *Harvard Business Review.* hbr.org/2016/02/a-refresher-on-statistical-significance.

Gartner, Inc (2018, 23 Feb). 'Fostering data literacy and information as a second language: A Gartner trend insight report.' emtemp.gcom.cloud/ngw/globalassets/en/doc/documents/3860965-fostering-data-literacy-and-information-as-a-second-language-a-gartner-trend-insight-report.pdf.

Glen, S (2021). 'Moving average: What it is and how to calculate it.' StatisticsHowTo.com. statisticshowto.com/probability-and-statistics/statistics-definitions/moving-average.

Graban, M (2019). *Measures of Success: React less, lead better, improve more.* Constancy, Inc.

Grant, A (2021). *Think Again: The power of knowing what you don't know.* Viking.

Hamilton, M (2017, 19 May). 'How to create value from business data.' PwC. pwc.com.au/digitalpulse/how-to-create-value-from-business-data.html.

Hancock, J (2015, 21 Aug). 'Trucking boss Peter Colbert jailed for more than 12 years over driver Robert Brimson's death.' ABC News. abc.net.au/news/2015-08-21/trucking-boss-peter-colbert-jailed-for-drivers-death/6714506.

Hand, DJ (2008). *Statistics: A very short introduction.* Oxford University Press.

Harford, T (2020). *How to Make the World Add Up: Ten rules for thinking differently about numbers.* Hachette.

Hastings, G, Stead, M & Webb, J (2004). 'Fear appeals in social marketing: Strategic and ethical reasons for concern.' *Psychology & Marketing, 21*(11), 961–986.

Heath, D & Heath, C (2011). *Switch: How to change things when change is hard.* Penguin.

Human Resources Today (2020, 15 Jan). 'Why employee engagement matters in compliance.' humanresourcestoday.com/compliance/employee-engagement.

iDashboards UK (2018, 28 Mar). 'People remember only 20% of what they read… But 80% of what they see.' medium.com/@iDashboards_UK/on-average-people-remember-only-20-of-what-they-read-but-80-of-what-they-see-8411224769e2.

Ismail, N (2019, 7 Mar). 'Extracting value from data: How to do it and the obstacles to overcome.' Information Age. information-age.com/extracting-value-from-data-123480490.

Jick, TD (1979). 'Mixing qualitative and quantitative methods: Triangulation in action.' *Administrative Science Quarterly, 24*(4), 602–611.

Jones, B (2018). '17 key traits of data literacy.' Data Literacy LLC. dataliteracy.com/wp-content/uploads/2019/02/17-Key-Traits-of-Data-Literacy-Spread-Layout.pdf

Jones, S & Pickett, M (2019). *Making the data-driven journey easy* [video]. Capgemini and Talend. vimeo.com/346075346.

Kahneman, D (2011). *Thinking, Fast and Slow.* Macmillan.

Kahneman, D, Knetsch, JL & Thaler, RH (1991). 'Anomalies: The endowment effect, loss aversion*, and status quo bias.' Journal of Economic Perspectives, 5*(1), 193–206.

Kappel, M (2020, 21 Jul). 'How to determine profit margin for your small business in 3 simple steps.' Patriot Software LLC. patriotsoftware.com/blog/accounting/how-do-you-determine-a-profit-margin.

Kermer, DA, Driver-Linn, E, Wilson, TD & Gilbert, DT (2006). 'Loss aversion is an affective forecasting error.' *Psychological Science, 17*(8), 649–653.

Klein, G & Jarosz, A (2011). 'A naturalistic study of insight.' *Journal of Cognitive Engineering and Decision Making,* 5(4), 335–351.

Knaflic, CN (2015). *Storytelling with Data: A data visualization guide for business professionals.* John Wiley & Sons.

Knaflic, CN (2020). 'The structure(s) of a story.' Storytelling with data. storytellingwithdata.com/blog/2020/5/21/the-structures-of-story.

Lencioni, P (2021, Mar). '83. Be a jerk' [Podcast episode]. At The Table with Patrick Lencioni. tablegroup.com/83-be-a-jerk.

Mejia, Z (2018, 19 Nov). 'Amazon's Jeff Bezos: This simple framework can help you answer the most difficult questions you face.' CNBC LLC. cnbc.com/2018/11/19/jeff-bezos-simple-strategy-for-answering-amazons-hardest-questions--.html

Melendez, C (2015, 4 Mar). 'Big data, big opportunity for Expedia and its customers.' InfoWorld. infoworld.com/article/2891702/big-data-big-opportunity-for-expedia-and-its-customers.html.

Mitroff, II & Sagasti, F (1973). 'Epistemology as general systems theory: An approach to the design of complex decision-making experiments.' *Philosophy of Social Sciences, 3*(2), 117–134.

Nickerson, RS (1998). 'Confirmation bias: A ubiquitous phenomenon in many guises.' *Review of General Psychology, 2*(2), 175–220.

Nottingham, J (2017). *The learning challenge: How to guide your students through the learning pit to achieve deeper understanding.* Corwin Press.

Petkosek, M & Moroney, W (2004). Human Factors and Ergonomics Society annual meeting proceedings: Guidelines for constructing graphs. Human Factors and Ergonomics Society. 45, pp. 1006–1009.

PwC (2021). 'PwC 24th annual global CEO survey.' pwc.com/gx/en/ceo-agenda/ceosurvey/2021/report.html.

Qlik (2019). *3rd generation business intelligence: Unlocking all the possibility in your data.* qlik.com/us/-/media/files/resource-library/global-us/register/whitepapers/wp-3rd-generation-bi-unlocking-all-the-possibility-in-your-data-en.pdf

Reuters Events (2017, 27 Apr). '3 ways data science is delivering for Expedia.' reutersevents.com/travel/revenue-and-data-management/3-ways-data-science-delivering-expedia.

Richardson, FC & Suinn, RM (1972). 'The mathematics anxiety rating scale: Psychometric data.' *Journal of Counselling Psychology, 19*(6), 551–554.

Rose, G (2001). *Visual methodologies: An introduction to the interpretation of visual materials.* SAGE Publications Inc.

Rosling, H with Rosling, O & Rönnlund, AR (2018). *Factfulness: Ten reasons we're wrong about the world – and why things are better than you think.* Hodder & Staughton.

Ross, L (1977). 'The intuitive psychologist and his shortcomings: Distortions in the attribution process.' In *Advances in Experimental Social Psychology* (Vol. 10, pp. 173-220). Academic Press.

Rozin, P & Royzman, EB (2001). 'Negativity bias, negativity dominance, and contagion.' *Personality and social psychology review, 5*(4), 296–320.

Ruhl, C (2021, 4 May). 'Cognitive bias examples.' Simply Psychology. simplypsychology.org/cognitive-bias.html.

Sapirstein, J (n.d.). *20 keys to building a data-driven culture.* Liftcentro.com. liftcentro.com/20-keys-to-building-a-data-driven-culture.

SAS Institute Inc (n.d.a.). 'Statistical knowledge portal – Correlation.' jmp.com/en_au/statistics-knowledge-portal/what-is-correlation.html.

SAS Institute Inc (n.d.b.). 'Statistical knowledge portal – Correlation versus causation.' jmp.com/en_au/statistics-knowledge-portal/what-is-correlation/correlation-vs-causation.html.

Seife, C (2010). *Proofiness: How you're being fooled by the numbers.* Penguin.

Sharma, A (2021). *Webinar: Data driven decision making by Expedia Sr PM, Akhil Sharma.* YouTube. youtube.com/watch?v=bNOcgpFi9iE.

Shepperd, J, Malone, W & Sweeny, K (2008). 'Exploring causes of the self-serving bias.' *Social and Personality Psychology Compass, 2*(2), 895–908.

Sinek, S (2009). *Start with Why: How great leaders inspire everyone to take action.* Penguin.

Sinek, S. (2019). *The Infinite Game.* Penguin.

Smale, W (2014, 24 Nov). 'The couple who helped transform the way we shop.' BBC News. bbc.com/news/business-30095454.

Tetlock, PE (1985). 'Accountability: A social check on the fundamental attribution error. *Social Psychology Quarterly*, 227–236.'

Thurmond, VA (2001). 'The point of triangulation.' *Journal of Nursing Scholarship, 33*(3), 253–258.

Tischler, R, Mack, M & Vitsenko, J (2017). *BARC research study: Interactive analytical storytelling.* sitsi.com/download/25919/185961/?ct=1.

Tufte, ER (2006). *Beautiful evidence.* Graphics Press.

Vigen, T (n.d.). 'Spurious correlations.' tylervigen.com/spurious-correlations.

Vora, S (2019). *The power of data storytelling* (1st ed.). Sage Publications.

Zhang, M (2020, 24 Dec). 'Inside the world's largest data center.' DgtlInfra. dgtlinfra.com/inside-the-worlds-largest-data-center.

About the author

Selena Fisk is a data storyteller who is passionate about helping others sort through the numbers to tell the real stories and lead positive change. She fiercely advocates for a world in which we are all data-informed, not data-driven; yet she realises that this isn't a skill set we all have or are confident in.

As a data coach and storyteller, Selena is as enthusiastic about building data storytelling skills in others as she is about building her own understanding of the evolving ways data can support individuals, organisations and communities to flourish and thrive. For Selena, using data in a way that benefits others is the only way to use it. Almost nothing will accelerate the impact we can have as humans like being able to see trends in the numbers, and using this information alongside our understanding of context to inform our decisions.

In her role as an independent data expert, Selena has mentored executive, senior and middle leaders as well as hundreds of others in data storytelling, positively impacting the organisations in which they work. With her background in teaching, she has developed resources to promote data storytelling in schools, including an online self-paced data storytelling course, and two books published by Hawker Brownlow Education and Solution Tree.

About the author

Acknowledgements

Books have a funny way of coming to fruition. The experiences I've had, the books and papers I've read, the people I've been lucky enough to work with and the people who support me all, in some way, shaped this little A5 book. It's never possible to mention everyone or everything that has contributed – after all, much of it isn't tangible – but I do know that I'm grateful for all of it.

I am particularly grateful for my tribe of extraordinary humans: Tim, Tash, Jhye, Darcy, Carly, Catherine, Mel, Liane, Al, Dan, Anna and Nicola. 'Thank you' just doesn't seem enough. JB, thanks for getting me out of my head (and house!) through the writing process and for reminding me to take life just that bit less seriously. #chickenfried

Thank you Lesley and Brooke for believing in the power of the numbers! You have both undoubtedly made this a better final product for the reader, so I also need to say thank you on their behalf.

To my TLBS tribe, particularly my writing quest groups and my BL Friday morning crew – you are absolute legends and I'm so glad we are on this journey together.

And finally, to the legends that I get to 'work' with on an ongoing basis – I love learning from you, working with you and being stretched by you. So much of this book has evolved because of you, and I am so grateful. Thank you.

Acknowledgements

Let's keep this conversation going!

Website: selenafisk.com

Email: selena@selenafisk.com

LinkedIn: Dr Selena Fisk

Twitter: @drselenafisk